CW00455349

SILENCE

SILENCE

A Series of Conferences
Given by a Camaldolese Hermit

Ercam Editions
Bloomingdale, Ohio
www.Camaldolese.org

Copyright © Holy Family Hermitage, 2011.
All rights reserved.

Cover: *St. Peter Martyr Enjoins Silence*,
      fresco painted c. 1441 by Bl. Fra Angelico.
      St. Mark Museum, Florence.

ISBN: 978-0-9728132-7-3

Printed in the United States of America

Contents

Introductory Conference

We begin a new cycle of conferences. In the last year we meditated for a long time on the Beatitudes of Our Lord and have seen that they are a manifestation of Christian Perfection. During Lent and after, we meditated on the recent documents of the Holy See which considered the contemplative life in the Church. It was an occasion for us to see more clearly where we are in the Church and what is the purpose of our vocation. We have seen the greatness of our vocation. We have seen how great are the expectations of God and His Church on our behalf.

We had more than one conference about Saint Romuald and Blessed Paul Giustiniani in order to come closer to our ideal as Camaldolese Hermits of Montecorona.

In the past we had a series of conferences on Saint Benedict. Today, before we come to our real theme, I would like to invite you once more to study privately the Rule of Saint Benedict with the help of a good commentary, and to go deeper and deeper into monastic spirituality. It is very important; it is a question of to be or not to be — are we monks and hermits with all our soul to the last consequences, able to make every sacrifice for Christ, or are we seeking ourselves, avoiding all sacrifices, especially humility and obedience, and heading towards failure and, perhaps, catastrophe in the future? We need strong spiritual food and strong attitudes in our way of life, a deep faith, and a spirit of sacrifice. We need a sound monastic formation.

Today we begin a long series of conferences about the spirit of silence. As we know, there is an exterior and an interior silence. Both are important for a life such as ours, but the interior silence is the more important. The exterior silence can be an expression of the interior silence, but often it can also be the expression of a sinful interior disposition, a lack of brotherly love, or the manifestation of an imperfect and self-centered soul.

We shall speak about the silence of our senses, about the silence of our interior faculties from the lowest to the highest.

In order to become men of prayer and men of God, we must give up everything, even our own judgment and our own will. All must be purified and entirely submitted to God. We cannot make any conditions with God, we cannot hold back for ourselves anything, still less impose our own will or our psychological disturbances upon others. Everything in us must be brought to silence, and only then will we be free for God and for the needs of others. We must strive toward purity of heart.

A silent man will be able to listen to the Holy Spirit and to follow His inspiration.

Silence, of course, is not an end in itself. It is only a means to something greater and more important. Silence cannot remain empty, for it must be filled with something greater, as for instance prayer, in all its forms, or the study of Divine Revelation, or prayerful work. Silence is vital in our life. It has a very deep meaning. If one day we lose the spirit of silence, then we will no longer be Camaldolese Hermits of Montecorona, nor men of prayer.

Silence is compatible with action. God is infinitely silent and infinitely active. All the universe, all mankind, and all creatures depend on Him. He takes care of all in greatest silence and peace, with infinite love. We also should learn to combine the spirit of silence with our daily occupations in such a way that we do not lose interior recollection or become noisy. We do all we are supposed to do.

Silence is compatible with joy. Silence should make us joyful. Our cell should become a paradise. It is a bad sign when silence makes us sad, when we begin to meditate on the complaints of our fallen nature instead of meditating on God and His infinite Love.

Silence is a challenge for all. Some become happy, some unhappy. In solitude and silence we can see what we really are, or better, who we really are.

It can be said that God loves silence. The mystery of the Incarnation was accomplished in greatest silence. In the Eucharist, where Christ is really present, He is the example of Christian Silence. Always substantially one with the Father, serving as Mediator between God and us, He becomes also the spiritual food for many. He is always ready to console and to help all those in need who have recourse to Him. O admirable Mystery, O most perfect example for all of us! In silence we should adore God and be united with Him; in silence we should pray and offer ourselves for the salvation of many; in silence we should be patient and bear all insults and offenses as Christ does in the Eucharist.

Our Blessed Mother is the singular and most perfect example of Christian silence. She spoke only a few words. She was always united with God but had her eyes and heart open to the needs of others [as at the wedding feast of Cana]¹. She is the perfect contemplative, adoring God in silence, and pondering all things in her heart.

Let us imitate Our Lord, the Blessed Virgin, and our holy Founders in their spirit of silence. Amen.

---

¹   Information in brackets — here and elsewhere — is supplied by the editor.

2

SILENCE OF THE EYES

In our introduction to the theme of silence, I announced a longer series of conferences about interior silence. We have seen that both are necessary, the interior and the exterior silence, but the former is the more important for our spiritual life. The silence of our tongue is important, but more important is the silence of our soul.

Today we shall speak about the silence of our eyes, what has been called in the past the custody of the eyes.

The eyes are the faculty to see. This faculty is certainly a great gift from God. But the Servant of God Josemaria Escriva de Balaguer, founder of Opus Dei [1902-1975, beatified in 1992 and canonized in 2002], in his book *The Way*[1], writes: "The eyes! Through them much wickedness enters into the soul. How many experiences like David's!"

"If you guard your eyes, you will be assured of guarding your heart."

As we can see, our gift of sight is not without danger. We have the faculty to see and to admire the beauty of creation and consequently to praise God. We also have the possibility of abusing our faculty to see and to offend God.

Tanquerey, in his book *The Spiritual Life*[2], warns us saying: "There are looks which are grievously sinful, that offend not only against modesty, but against chastity itself; from such we must

---

[1] *The Way,* Scepter Publishers, 1979.
[2] *The Spiritual Life*, Desclée & Co., 1930.

evidently abstain." Tanquerey continues: "Others there are which are dangerous; for instance, to fasten our eyes on persons or things which would of themselves be apt to bring on temptations."

Tanquerey writes also that "the earnest Christian who wants to save his soul at all costs, mortifies the sense of sight by repressing idle, curious glances and by duly controlling his eyes in all simplicity, without any show of affectation."

We could continue to quote many good authors who teach us how to avoid dangers because of the lack of mortification of the eyes, and how to control our sight. But we shall no longer make quotations.

As we know, our exterior senses communicate their impressions to our soul, and if we are not vigilant enough we will not be sufficiently recollected for our life of prayer. What is more, we will not become true contemplatives if we give total freedom to our eyes, to our curiosity.

I do not say that we should always have closed eyes or that we should only look towards heaven. It would not be possible or prudent. All we have to do is to put our eyes to good use. There will be times when we should say "no" to our curiosity in the desire to see everything. There will be times when we should say "yes" to our eyes, but always in a prayerful seeking.

The last time, I mentioned that Our Lady, at the wedding feast in Cana, saw that there was no more wine. We also should see the needs of others, the needs of our community, and be ready to help where help is necessary.

It is amazing how some people see everything and find what they desire to have for themselves, but they cannot see the needs of others.

I remember, for it has happened, that new candidates came to our office and looked without modesty on all they saw. They even took letters or books to satisfy their curiosity. That we should not do! There are limits beyond which we should never go. The mortification of our eyes, as mortification in other matters, is very important for our spiritual life. There must be a discipline in our life, an ascetical exercise.

Very often, the desire to see everything, to read everything, to satisfy all curiosity, can have deep roots in our soul, in our unmortified ego! It could be an indication of immaturity, or even of a psychological disorder.

The contemplative must give up many things in order to become recollected, to become a man of prayer. We have no television, no movies, no secular periodicals or newspapers that could hinder our spirit of recollection and prayer.

We should avoid all kinds of reading which would distract us or make prayer more difficult. We should not be worldly-minded or earthly-minded even under the pretext of study or science. If a study is not bringing us to God, if it makes prayer more difficult or impossible, such study is not for us hermits as men of prayer. Our soul should never be the receptacle of trash. We are a temple of the Holy Spirit, the Most Holy Trinity lives in us!

Our exterior silence, the silence of our tongue, will be an authentic silence if it proceeds from a silent and mortified soul. Our soul will be silent if we bring to silence our senses, our passions, and all the faculties of our soul.

If our silence proceeds from a silent soul, if it is from a mortified soul, it will not be an empty silence. If Christ really becomes the life of our soul, our silence as well as our speaking will be filled with the spirit of God. Then there will be nothing artificial or pharisaical, only simplicity and naturalness.

The action of the Holy Spirit, in purifying our soul and making it Christ-like, will enable us to be united with God, and tell us when we should speak, as well as when to keep silence.

The silence of our eyes, for the sake of deeper union with God, will become very helpful for our spiritual life.

On the contrary, the lack of mortification of our eyes — the restless eyes, the curious eyes, the selfish eyes — can become a greater obstacle in our union with God, in our prayer life, and indeed, an obstacle to becoming contemplative souls.

Experiences like David's with Bathsheba, the wife of Uriah, do not belong only to the past. They happen also today. Really, no one should be too sure of himself and give full license to his eyes. We know that among consecrated men and women, even bishops, monks, and hermits, some abandoned their first love and became married. We are living in a time of great permissiveness, when all seems to be licit and justified. No wonder that so many fall into the snares of the devil.

"Watch ye and pray that you enter not into temptation. The spirit indeed is willing, but the flesh is weak" — said Our Lord to the Apostles who accompanied Him during the Agony at Gethsemane.

These same words Our Lord is addressing to us, to all consecrated souls: "Be on guard and pray."

*   *   *

Before I finish our conference, I would like to say something about our eyes. Being in a seminary more than fifty years ago, I read a book of Cardinal Bertram addressed to priests. "There are two things which we cannot hide," said the German Cardinal, "that is, our voice and our eyes." Let us ask, why is this so?

The voice and eyes will betray us if we are sincere or not, whether we are saying the truth or not. In our eyes people can see if we are angry or fearful — the same in the voice — if we are proud or humble, or if we are sad or joyful. The eyes will tell if our heart is pure or full of lust and other things.

Let us remember the words of Our Lord: "The lamp of the body is the eye. It follows that if the eye is sound, your whole body will be filled with light. But if the eye is diseased, your whole body will be all darkness. If then, the light inside you is darkness, what darkness will that be!" (Mt 6:22)

The eyes are not only the door from the outside into our soul, they are also the expression of the depth of the soul itself to the outside, to all that we look at.

I hope that we see better how important it is to have a good control over our eyes, to let only good impressions enter into our soul. On the other hand, if our soul is pure and mortified, our eyes will be the expression of God living and acting in us.

May Our Lord help us to make good use of the precious gift of sight. Amen.

3

SILENCE OF HEARING (PART 1)

We continue our reflections on silence. Everything within us, as well as our senses, should be brought to silence in order to listen to the Holy Spirit and to become more and more united with Christ.

Last week we spoke about the silence of our eyes, of our curiosity, and so forth. Today we shall speak about our hearing. We shall reflect on the great gift of God which enables us to hear, to listen. We shall also see how this faculty can be abused, and finally, what our attitude as Christians and as monks or hermits in listening to God should be.

May the Holy Spirit be our guide.

The sense of hearing is a great gift from God. The very construction of our ear (external and internal) is a little masterpiece, a sign and manifestation of the wisdom and omnipotence of God.

The ears are given to us to enable us to hear as the eyes are given to us to see. Both hearing and sight are of great importance in the development of a child, of a man, of all of us.

Today we shall speak about the precious gift of hearing which enables us to listen to the voice of nature and to the voice of others. We have two ears but only one tongue. That means we should listen more than we talk. The ears also give balance to our body. A defect in hearing can cause us to lose our balance.

We could continue meditating on the sense of hearing as a great gift of God and give praise and thanks to the Almighty Creator for this precious faculty to hear. Please God, that we never abuse this gift! Let us always remember the admonitions of Saint James, "my dear brothers: be quick to listen but slow to speak." (Jas 1:19)

Man has the tremendous gift of freedom and, consequently, the possibility of saying "yes" or "no" to God.

All gifts received from God on the natural level, as well as on the supernatural level, can be used for the glory of God and the salvation of souls. But all the gifts, without exception, can also be abused.

The gift of hearing, as we know, can work in two directions. On the one hand, as Saint Paul writes to the Romans: "Faith comes through hearing, and what is heard is the word of Christ." (Rom 10:17) Consequently, our growth in faith, our spiritual formation, comes also in great part through hearing. On the other hand, the temptations of the devil can come through listening to his seductive voice. Being the Father of Lies, he will tell us lies in order to deceive and conquer us. In the first temptation mentioned in the Holy Scripture, the devil said to Eve: "No! you will not die! God knows in fact, on the day you eat it, your eyes will be opened and you will be like gods, knowing good and evil." (Gn 3:4ff) We know all the rest. Because Eve and Adam listened to the voice of the devil, the worst things happened and still continue in the world.

Even today the devil is at work. He has conquered many allies, many cooperators, and the means of communication, in order to contradict the voice of God and the voice of the Church. Also, the voice of all legitimate authority is questioned, and finally, the voice of our consciences is dulled. Indeed, we can see the fruits of the devil's action in the world and on the human face of the Church. We see the numerous victims of diabolic seduction.

The evils of our days come because men are rather inclined to listen to lies of the devil, rather than to the Eternal Truth, to Our Lord Jesus Christ Himself.

We know that the final victory belongs to Christ and to His followers. But how many millions of our brothers and sisters are yet to become victims of the devil, listening all too easily to him and to his representatives on all human levels?

What should be our attitude as Christians and as hermits? Saint Peter in his last letter asks us to resist the devil, to be strong in faith: "Stay sober and alert, your opponent, the devil, is prowling like a roaring lion looking for someone to devour. Resist him, solid in your faith." (1 Pt 5:8-9)

Here is the first point: Christians should be on their guard against the snares of the devil. In order to do so, we need a deep faith. Unfortunately, many are losing their faith, and consequently they become careless and weak. They no longer can, nor do, resist the devil. This is the beginning of the end for many.

Secondly: We should listen to the voice of God and follow His admonitions. From the beginning of human life on earth, God has spoken to mankind in various ways. He addressed Himself in a special way to the Chosen People, to the descendants of Abraham, Isaac, and Jacob. He spoke to us most perfectly through His Eternal Son, who became man, Our Lord Jesus Christ. In Christ, eternity broke into time and heaven came to earth.

Jesus said of Himself: "Everyone who listens to these words of mine and acts on them, will be like a sensible man who has built his house on rock... but everyone who listens to these words of mine and does not act on them, will be like a stupid man who has built his house on sand." (Mt 7:24ff)

Here, my Brothers, lies one of the main reasons why many have lost the path to salvation. They were overcome by the evil one. Instead of following Christ, they followed the voice of fallen nature, victims of the devil.

The cosmic struggle between Christ and the devil, between good and evil, is a vital reality and we all must make our own choice. Either we are with Christ, or we are against Christ, with all the consequences!

The third point: The logical consequence of what has been said above is this: every voice coming to us must be tested. This is what is called discernment of the spirits.

Saint John the Apostle, in his first letter writes: "Beloved, do not trust every spirit, but put the spirits to a test to see if they belong to

God, because many false prophets have appeared in the world." (1 Jn 4:1)

We live in times of great confusion. There are a number of theologians, priests, and religious sisters who are in open opposition to the teaching of the Church. There are many abuses, many errors obstinately defended and shamelessly propagated.

Also, the crimes of abortion and the sinful disease of divorce, as well as other transgressions of the Commandments of God, are carried out as though normal and harmless. In these situations we should remember what Saint Peter said to the Apostles: "Obedience to God comes before obedience to men." (Acts 5:29)

We should also remember what Our Lord said: "Beware of false prophets who come to you disguised as sheep, but underneath are ravenous wolves. You will be able to tell them by their fruit...a sound tree produces good fruit but a rotten tree produces bad fruit... Any tree that does not produce good fruit is cut down and thrown on the fire." (Mt 7:15-20)

*   *   *

The next time we shall continue our reflections on the same theme, going more deeply into our life as hermits. We shall see that we should bring to silence all voices which do not come from God, to be able to listen to the Holy Spirit and follow His promptings. Amen.

4

Silence of Hearing (part 2)

In our last conference we spoke about the silence of our sense of hearing. Today we shall continue our reflections on the same theme, going deeper into our life as hermits. We shall see that we should bring to silence all voices which do not come from God or from His representatives and be able to listen entirely to the Holy Spirit and to follow His promptings.

*   *   *

Let us see first of all what the Holy Scripture says about our duty to God and the advantages of listening to God. We will also go to Saint Benedict and see what he says in the Holy Rule about listening. Further, we shall profit by the experience of others in the same manner.

*   *   *

The Holy Scripture has many passages about listening, too many even to consider them all in our conferences. The Concordance to the Bible has eighteen pages of references to the words "to hear" and "to hearken." The *Theological Dictionary of the New Testament* has nine pages about hearing or listening. Among other things from the Old Testament we read, "The decisive religious statement is: Hear the

13

Word of the Lord." (Is 1:10; Jer 2:4; Am 7:16) "Hear, O heavens, and give ear, O earth: for the Lord speaks." (Is 1:2) On the other hand, the decisive accusation is that of failure or "unwillingness to hear." (Jer 7:13; Hos 9:17)

Throughout the New Testament — continues the same author — "hearing is strongly emphasized, to some degree almost more so than seeing." (Mk 4:24; Mt 11:4, 13:13-16; Lk 2:20; Acts 2:33; 1 Jn 1:1)

"The extent of hearing is determined by the content of the messages. In the New Testament this is always the offering of salvation and ethical demand in one. Hearing is then always the reception both of grace and of the call to repentance. This means that the only marks to distinguish true hearing are faith and action, their crown is the concept of obedience." (Kittel, in the *Theological Dictionary of the New Testament*)

I would like to rest a little and ponder for a short while three characteristic texts about the attitude of listening as expressed in the Holy Scripture.

First of all, let us listen to the voice of the heavenly Father speaking at the Transfiguration of Our Lord, "This is my beloved Son on whom my favor rests. Listen to him." (Mt 17:5) God spoke to the Apostles, but His message is destined for all men; also for us. We have to listen to Christ in order to be saved. Christ was teaching us during His earthly life. He continues to teach us through the Holy Spirit and through those who represent Christ on earth — through the Church.

The coming and role of the Holy Spirit was foretold by Our Lord Himself. In John we read: "When he comes, being the Spirit of truth, he will guide you to all truth. He will not speak on his own, but will speak only what he hears, and will announce to you the things to come. In doing this he will give glory to me, because he will have received from me what he will announce to you." (Jn 16:13ff)

Christ speaks also to us through the Church and through those who received authority from Him, such as Superiors in the religious life and parents in family life. Christ said of them, "Who listens to you listens to me — he who hears you, hears me. He who rejects you, rejects me. And he who rejects me rejects him who sent me." (Lk 10:16) At the Transfiguration the heavenly Father said of Christ, "This is my beloved Son, listen to him." Christ said: "He who rejects me" — (directly, or in my representatives) — "rejects him who sent me, the Father." Here is a very important point. If we listen to Christ and to His representatives on earth, we are on the path to salvation. If we reject them, we risk our own salvation to the perdition of our souls.

The second text on which I would like to meditate a little is found in James 1:22: "You must do what the word tells you, and not just listen to it and deceive yourself." In another translation we read, "Be doers of the word and not hearers only, deceiving your own selves." In Matthew 7:24 we read: "It is not those who say to me, 'Lord, Lord,' who will enter the Kingdom of heaven, but the person who does the will of my Father in heaven." In Luke 8:21 we find, "My mother and my brothers are those who hear the words of God and put it into practice." Saint Paul wrote to the Romans: "It is not listening to the Law, but keeping it that will make people holy in the sight of God." (Rom 2:13)

I think those references from Scripture should be enough to understand how important it is that we be not only hearers, but also doers. In our last conference I quoted Jesus saying of Himself: "Everyone who listens to the words of mine and acts on them, will be like a sensible man who built his house on rock...but everyone who listens to these words of mine and does not act on them, will be like a stupid man who built his house on sand. Rain came down, floods rose, gales blew and struck that house, and it fell, and what a fall it had." (Mt 7:24-27) In another translation we read, "And great was the fall of it."

The third text of the Holy Scripture on which we should briefly meditate, is found in Psalm 94: "Today, listen to the voice of the Lord: do not grow stubborn, as your fathers did in the wilderness."

In Hebrews (3:7-19) we find a comment on the quoted passage of Psalm 94. We read there: "The Holy Spirit says, 'If only you would listen to him today...' Take care brothers, that there is not in any one

15

of your communities a wicked mind, so unbelieving as to turn away from the living God. Every day, as long as this 'today' lasts, keep encouraging one another so that none of you is hardened by the lure of sin, because we shall remain coheirs with Christ only if we keep a grasp on our first confidence right to the end."

*   *   *

In the Prologue and in the Rule of Saint Benedict [RB] we find many references as to how we have to listen in the monastic life. We are told: we should listen to God, to the Holy Scripture, to the Abbot, to the Rule. We are even invited right from the beginning of the Prologue, to listen carefully to the master's instructions, and attend to them with the ear of our heart.

What does this mean "with the ear of our heart?" It is an image, of course, because the heart has no ear. But here we find expressed a very deep truth. We should not only listen with our ears, but with our heart, with a loving and docile heart. "The labor of obedience" — says Saint Benedict — "will bring you back to him from whom you drifted through the sloth of disobedience." (Prologue 2)

Saint Benedict quotes, also, the Holy Scripture. He reminds us of the above mentioned Psalm 94: "If you hear his voice today, do not harden your hearts."

Speaking about obedience, Saint Benedict says: "The obedience shown to superiors is given to God, as he himself said, 'Whoever listens to you, listens to me.'" (Lk 10:16) [RB 5]

Saint Benedict says also that we should not only be listeners, but also doers; he quotes Matthew 7:24-25: "Whoever hears these words of mine and does them is like a wise man who built his house upon rock."

In Chapter 4, "On the Instruments of Good Works," Saint Benedict invites us to listen readily to holy readings and devote ourselves often to prayer.

*   *   *

In the beginning of our conference I announced that we would see today what the Holy Scripture and Saint Benedict say about listening, and I added we would also profit from the experience of others in the same matter.

Whom should I quote? There are so many who could teach us how to listen to God, to Christ and His Church, and to all who take the place of God on earth.

I think, *The Following of Christ* [*The Imitation of Christ*, by Thomas à Kempis] is a good book to open now. In the third book there are at least three chapters about listening:

1. of preparing one's soul to listen to Christ speaking within;
2. that the truth speaks inwardly without the sound of words;
3. that we must listen to the word of God with humility.

Not having the necessary time today to read here the three chapters, I will ask you to read the first three chapters of the third book of *The Following of Christ*.

"Speak, Lord, for Thy servant heareth." (1 Sam 3:9) Amen.

5

SILENCE OF TASTE

This is our fifth conference on Silence. Today we shall speak about the silence of our sense of taste in one aspect.

As in all senses in general, so also our taste is a gift from God. We receive it for some good purposes, but as with all other senses, so our taste can be abused in two directions, by two opposite extremes.

Taste is given to us to enjoy the gifts of God: food and drink which we daily receive. Taste is also, in many cases, a safeguard for our health.

The author of *The Spiritual Combat,*[1] Dom Lawrence Scupoli, writes: "When you taste something pleasing to your palate, consider that God alone is capable of giving it that relish so agreeable to you; place in him all your delight, and say within yourself: 'O my soul rejoice, that as without God there can be no solid content, so in him all happiness is found.'" (p. 81) St. Francis de Sales, for more than twenty years carried this book in his pocket and every day read some passages of it.

Gluttony is the abuse of that legitimate pleasure God has attached to eating and drinking, which are necessary means of self-preservation.

Tanquerey, in his book *The Spiritual Life,* says that "gluttony is an inordinate love of the pleasures of the table. The disorder lies in pursuing this satisfaction for its own sake, in considering it, either

---

[1]   *The Spiritual Combat*, Catholic Book Publishing Co., 1951.

explicitly or implicitly as an end in itself, as do those 'whose god is their belly' (Phil 3:19); or in pursuing the said delight to excess, at times even to the detriment of health, by disregarding the rules of sobriety."

Cassian, in his book called *The Institutes*, has forty-one chapters on the Spirit of Gluttony. It would be very interesting and of great use for our spiritual life, if we could read them all and reflect upon them. There is great wisdom in the sayings of the Fathers on this subject.

Cassian, in one of his *Conferences*, said that the eagle is at peace and in security as long as he flies very high. The danger arrives when the eagle comes lower in search of food. He can be caught or killed. So also, continues Cassian, the monk or hermit must restore his body with food and drink. He can be easily caught by the devil through lack of mortification and through the spirit of gluttony.

We know, as Saint Paul teaches us, that "the kingdom of God does not mean eating or drinking this or that." (Rom 14:17) Or another translates it, "The Reign of God is not a matter of eating and drinking" — but we know also by experience how much can be lost from our spiritual life because of our wrong attitudes, or by our lack of mortification in the matter of food and drink.

The spirit of gluttony is very subtle and has deep roots in our fallen nature. Many times, we are not even aware of our spiritual infirmity; we try to justify by all means that we are right, and we behave as if our vices were great virtues and a matter of great prudence and wisdom.

Mortification at table is the ABC of all mortification, and as Cassian puts it, quoting blessed Macarius, "a monk ought to bestow attention on his fasts, as if he were going to remain in the flesh for a hundred years." (Ch. 41) During all our life, we must be aware of the dangers of gluttony and of the necessity of moderation and mortification in this matter. Following Saint Benedict, we should "love fasting" (RB 4.13) and "refrain from too much eating," (4.36) "nor be given to wine." (4.35)

"Theologians point out four different ways" — says Tanquerey — "in which we may violate these rules:

1. Eating when there is no need for it, nor other reason than that of indulging our greed.
2. Seeking delicacies or daintily prepared food, the more to enjoy their relish.
3. Going beyond either appetite or need, gorging oneself with food or drink with danger to health.
4. Eating with avidity, with greed, after the manner of certain animals. This fashion of eating is considered ill-mannered by the world."

Let us reflect a little upon the four ways of violating sobriety and moderation in eating and drinking.

The first point was eating when there is no need: for instance, eating between meals.

Here we could make a distinction between real and imaginary needs, between physical or physiological needs and psychological ones.

There is a basic difference between a tired hard-worker sitting down to eat and a psychologically unbalanced man who is finicky about what he should eat and what he should avoid. The former will restore his body and will fulfill the will of God. The latter is very often doing great harm to his own health, increasing also his psychological disturbances and preoccupations.

I remember that in Colombia we rarely had fish due to not having a freezer. We received daily two eggs at noon. One novice, sickly and psychologically unsettled, ate only the yolks. He regularly threw out the rest to the hungry birds which came to visit him. After a year and a half, the brother left exhausted. We learned from the doctor that the brother discarded what would have been of great use in his particular case. Very often people make their own judgment and eat what they like and throw out what they dislike.

Eating between meals has a long history, even in the eremitical life. If in the case of lay people the transgression in this matter is a lack of moderation and mortification, in the case of a hermit, eating between meals without permission can become a very dangerous thing. He could easily be caught by the devil, who later on will ask other and greater concessions from him, leading to relaxation of observance and spiritual ruin.

Msgr. Josemaria Escriva de Balaguer wrote that gluttony is the forerunner of impurity. A similar thought was expressed by Father Janvier (Lent, 1921), a famous preacher. He said: "Excess in eating and drinking paves the way to unchastity, the offspring of gluttony." (Tanquerey, p. 412)

The second consideration of Tanquerey to be absolutely avoided, is seeking delicacies, special food daintily prepared, so as to enjoy more their relish.

In my own experience many things could be said here. It is more than probable that a hermit will not go to first-class restaurants for gourmet and fancy foods. But there are other ways of seeking one's own satisfaction. Normally they go in two directions. In the first place, some people are not satisfied with the nourishment they receive. They do not eat what they do not like. They often murmur and complain. They can become psychologically ill and unhappy. Later on they start asking for other and better food and drink. They create artificial needs in others and have the gift to procure for themselves what they think they need.

It is possible that these manifestations are a reaction against a careless or unbalanced diet served in some communities. It can also be a subtle expression of selfishness, of a lack of mortification, and can possibly be based in gluttony.

As much as it depends on me, I try to assure the community of a healthy and sufficient diet. In the kitchen, I try to serve Christ in my brothers. We also have special days of common refectory [*tristegas*] where, on special occasions, we serve finer food and even exceptional drinks such as wine or beer. All that together has a deeper psychological meaning. I also try to understand the needs of others and I avoid, as much as possible, imposing on others my likes and dislikes.

The purpose of our conferences on silence is precisely to silence all voices in us which are not coming from God, but arise from our fallen nature or even from the devil.

Let us reflect a little and see if we use the sense of taste for the glory of God, and our self-preservation in order to serve God and be able to fulfill all our duties. Let us see if we bring to silence our inordinate appetites, if we are masters of our likes and dislikes in matters of food and drink, if we are following the advice of Saint Paul: "Whether you eat or drink do all for the glory of God." (1 Cor 10:31)

6

SILENCE OF THE APPETITE

Last Saturday we spoke about our sense of taste, of its use and of its possible abuse. Following Tanquerey, we enumerated four different ways in which the spirit of sobriety and moderation can be violated.

We spoke also about eating when there is no need for it and of seeking delicacies and daintily prepared food. Today we shall speak about the last two vices in eating and continue our meditation on the silence of our sense of taste.

Tanquerey says going beyond either appetite or need, gorging oneself with food or drink with danger to health, is the third way of violating sobriety and moderation.

Last week we spoke about the qualitative abuse about seeking delicacies and fancy food. We come now to the quantity of food, how much should we eat.

Let us say right from the beginning that the need of food and drink differs from one person to another. Everyone has his own needs and should be given food according to his needs. In the Acts of the Apostles we read: "Distribution was made to each one as he had need." (Acts 4:35) St. Benedict makes the following comment: "Whoever needs less should thank God and not be distressed, but whoever needs more should feel humble because of his weakness, not self-important because of the kindness shown him. In this way all the members will be at peace." (RB 34)

We have mentioned before that there can be real or imaginary needs, physiological or psychological ones. All that should be taken into consideration. It will not always be easy to find the golden mean between two opposite extremes, to be virtuous in eating and drinking and not going to excesses.

You will find some people who will say of themselves that they are eating too much, when really they do not eat enough according to their needs. Consequently, great discretion should be observed in the matter of fasting and deprivation of certain foods. Some will say of themselves that they are eating very little, when in reality they are eating too much.

It can also occur that some people will not eat what they receive, saying it is too much, but at the same time they will be great consumers of special foods such as peanut butter, honey, cheese, pies, fruit or bread. The same thing will happen with drink — they will be enemies of wine or beer, of coffee or tea, but they will drink milk in unusual amounts. We can also eat little and still be unmortified, as was a man who told me he drank thirty cans of beer every day.

The last point mentioned by Tanquerey as an abuse is eating with avidity, with greed. He says this fashion of eating is considered by the world as "ill-mannered." Could such abuses happen in the religious life? All we know is that where there are human beings, there are also human weaknesses. I remember two cases that shocked me. The first happened in an abbey that I visited. I received coffee with cookies from a Brother. He ate almost all the cookies himself. I had the impression that the poor man rarely received cookies and he took advantage of the first occasion presented to him.

The second was a sad event also. A religious Brother liked sugar so much that it became a real vice. He could give up many things, but not sugar. When the community took coffee after lunch, the Brother took so much sugar and with such avidity that I felt embarrassed for him. My personal reaction was an examination of conscience; I asked myself if I might have a similar vice and not be aware of it. It can be wine, beer, coffee, honey, candies, and many other things of which we are not aware, but which could cause astonishment and even scandal.

In some instances I should mention that the monastic kitchen can be a source of suffering and of additional penances. Imagine the situation where there is no competent cook, or where the cook is careless, or other situations; for example, where the cook has little to offer, as was the case in our hermitage in Colombia. For St. Bernard, going to the refectory was always a great penance, partly because of his bad health.

Permit me to enumerate some good principles which should help us in our own life:

1. We did not come to a hermitage to eat well. But we should eat in such a way so as to be able to serve God and to perform our duties well.
2. We should eat and drink as much as we really need and are permitted by our Rule or Constitutions.
3. It is good, says Tanquerey, to eat always a little of something we dislike.
4. As there should be no day in our normal life without eating or drinking, so there should also be no day in our life without a little mortification at table. "The day you leave the table without having made some small mortification, you will have eaten as a pagan" — says Msgr. Josemaria Escriva de Balaguer. (*The Way*, p. 158)
5. Let us be happy with all we receive and never complain about food.
6. Some practical rules for the cook:
   a. The cook is obliged in conscience to be clean and to do his job well.
   b. There should be a great simplicity and variety in the diet, which should be balanced and healthy.
   c. The cook should not follow his own likes and dislikes, but serve his Brothers as Christ Himself in the person of his Brothers.

d. In our life the cook should follow our Constitutions and allow others to be good hermits as far as sobriety and moderation goes, but also give what is required and necessary for health.

Now some quotations from the Desert Fathers:

"Abba Poeman said: 'We have not been taught to kill our bodies, but to kill our passions.'"

"The same also said: 'There are three things which I am not able to do without: food, clothing and sleep, but I can restrict them to some extent.'"

"Abba Poeman heard of someone who had gone all week without eating and then had lost his temper. The old man said: 'He could do without food for six days, but he could not cast out anger.'"

"Abba Poeman also said: 'In Abba Pambo we see three bodily activities: abstinence from food until the evening, silence, and much manual work.'"

"Syncletica said: 'When you have to fast do not pretend illness. For those who do not fast often fall into real sickness.'"

"Someone said to Abba Arsenius: 'My thoughts trouble me, saying "You can neither fast nor work, at least go and visit the sick for that is also charity." But the old man, recognizing the suggestions of the demons, said to him, "Go eat, drink, sleep, do no work, only do not leave your cell." For he knew that steadfastness in the cell keeps a monk in the right way.'"

We make an end to our reflections on this subject. Let us remember that we have the duty to control our appetites and to bring to silence our imaginary needs. Let us make good use of the nourishment given by God to keep us in good health and enable us to serve God with all our strength and to fulfill our mission on earth. Moderation and sobriety will be our guidelines. Let us imitate Our Lord in this regard also.

Amen.

7

Silence of Touch (part 1)

Today we shall speak about our sense of touch. As we know, the lack of mortification of this sense could have disastrous consequences for our spiritual life. Many have left their first love for God and have given up everything because they could not dominate their passions nor mortify their sense of touch. Usually evil enters our soul by more than one door, but the sense of touch creates special difficulties. It promises great carnal pleasures which, of course, are only passing and of short duration. But they diminish strength of soul and create a state of spiritual weakness, and excite always more and more the desire for illicit pleasures which lead to spiritual ruin.

When we consider our sense of touch, we see that in all of us there exists a dormant tendency to seek commodities for our body and to avoid all which could make us suffer. We have the tendency to sit on a comfortable chair and in a comfortable manner. By nature we try to avoid all sacrifice and all mortification. We do not like to be sick. We do not like to suffer the heat of summer or the cold of winter. The voice of our fallen nature will tell us we should be as comfortable as possible.

By nature we do not like disagreeable or heavy work. We do not like to perspire.

But in the light of faith, on the supernatural level, things seem to be quite different. First of all, we must learn also that the sense of touch is a gift of God and was granted us for a good purpose.

Through our touch we can both accomplish great things and avoid many dangers.

Imagine the work of a physician, especially of a surgeon, or the accomplishment of artists such as sculptors, painters, and musicians. Look also on the patient work of nurses, tailors, typists, mechanics, gardeners, and many others. See how great a gift is the sense of touch! Through touch, by the will of God, is made the procreation of mankind. Through touch we can also avoid dangers. We can distinguish hot from cold, hard from soft, the agreeable from the painful, and so many other things. Consequently, we should be grateful to God for the precious gift of touch and make the best use of it in our life.

Unfortunately, as with all other senses and gifts, so also the sense of touch can be abused. As mentioned, instead of glorifying God, we can offend God, not doing the right things.

I mentioned that our fallen nature is more inclined to abuse the gifts of God than to make right use of them. I mentioned likewise that we have the tendency to avoid sacrifices and to assure our body all possible comforts. But in the light of faith, on the supernatural level, we learn how wrong and imperfect we can be.

I would like to treat some practical points which should enable us to see better what we have to do and what we should avoid in order to become good Christians, and good Camaldolese, making best use of the gift of touch.

In the first place, if we have received some special gifts or skills, let us be grateful to God and use them for the glory of God. In our life of course, it would be impossible to become a good musician, or even an artist. It would also be impossible to become a physician, still less a surgeon. But many other things are possible and allowed in a Camaldolese hermitage. How fortunate is the community where there are men who can exercise one or more crafts. We had Brothers and still have some, being really gifted by God, who have been very useful for the common good. In our life we are under obedience, and also our work must remain under obedience. We shall often have occasions to bring to silence our tendency to accomplish something if that is not permitted by our representative of God, or not in harmony with our way of life approved by the Church and the expression of the will of God.

We should be ready to make good use of all gifts received from God, but we should even be more ready to do always and only the will of God.

In our hermitage we need qualified people for diverse works. Sometimes our candidates know many things when they arrive because of their studies and experience in the world. More often, however, they learn many things at the hermitage. In former times the older Brothers introduced the young ones to many practical works and communicated to them their wisdom and experience.

In this hermitage we do not have old and experienced Brothers. But let us hope we soon will have good vocations and together be able to accomplish things which are necessary in our common, but eremitical life.

In the second place I would like to speak about our attitudes towards the comforts of modern life.

It is well known that monks and hermits in the past always had a preference for austerities and not for an easy life. They were mortified in soul and in body. They slept on the ground and had a stone for a pillow. They ate very little and were happy. They spent many hours in prayers and vigils, depriving themselves of well merited rest. They always were busy. Their conversion was sincere and irrevocable.

St. Benedict mitigated this excessive zeal for austerities, but he preserved the genuine spirit of Christian mortification.

St. Romuald and Bl. Paul Giustiniani have given us the teaching and the example of great austerities, but they also have taught us the primacy and preeminence of Christian love above all other things.

I remember when I visited Father Ambrose, a former Major of our Congregation who also had been my Novice Master. It was at Nola, in 1968, and I asked him to give me some advice for the future. After a night of reflection, he gave me three points as guidelines. Among these, he said: "Preserve always the austerities of our life."

I have tried to be faithful to the advice of my former novice Master, Father Ambrose, who died in 1972.

I realize also that austerities are not an end in themselves, but only a means to perfection. However, through the experience of my whole life, I have come to the conclusion that mortification in general, and austerity of life in particular, are necessary and very helpful in every Christian life, and indispensable in the life of a hermit. The Camaldolese way of life requires great abnegation and readiness to embrace the Cross whenever it may appear on our way to heaven. We need something better and stronger than an easy life. We must deeply share in the Paschal mystery of Christ, in His death and Resurrection. With all that in mind, we should not look as to how we can become free of all burden and all inconveniences. We should not fear to embrace wholeheartedly the difficulties and hardships of our life, nor be afraid to suffer a little. Our way of life, manner of sleeping, of dressing, of work, the way we pray in the church, standing or kneeling, and so forth, will give us many occasions to bring to silence the voice of our fallen nature which asks for comfort and ease. Through our vow of conversion of manners we are reminded that we should walk in the light of faith and live the new life. It is the life of Christ, the Crucified and Risen Lord. Many things will become easier to endure and even agreeable to bear in the measure we grow in love. All our austerities, all our abnegations and deprivations should prepare the way to perfect love and to a prayerful life.

I have not finished. Next time we shall continue our reflections in the same line and among other things, we shall speak about hygiene and our attitude in face of pain and sickness.

May the example of Our Lord inspire us to follow Him, bearing joyfully our crosses and austerities. May His love and His grace strengthen us, give us courage and perseverance to the end.

Amen.

8

SILENCE OF TOUCH (PART 2)

This is our eighth conference on silence. We continue to meditate upon our sense of touch. We shall ask ourselves how we can bring to silence the unjustified and unmortified demands of our fallen nature, especially our sense of touch.

In our last conference, we spoke about some practical points and began to examine some of our attitudes towards the comforts of modern life. We came to the conclusion that hermits, especially in our day, should not have an easy life, nor be afraid to suffer because of the hardships and austerities of our life. We mentioned, also, that all our austerities and abnegations should prepare us for perfect love and for a prayerful life.

I think it is clear that all followers of Christ, and especially hermits, should imitate Our Lord in His attitudes towards the comforts of earthly life. His case was extreme: He was born in a grotto, in a place destined for animals. In Nazareth, He had a very ordinary life without earthly comforts, a life of simplicity and hard work. During His public life He did not have a home or even a room which He could call His own. We remember His words: "Foxes have holes and the birds of the air have nests, but the Son of Man has nowhere to lay his head." (Mt 8:20; Lk 9:58) Christ died on the cross, naked, humiliated, abandoned, accepting His Passion and death out of love for His heavenly Father and for all men. He redeemed us and made satisfaction for all our sins. There were the sins of our lack of mortification, of the sense of touch, and the unhealthy search for an easy and comfortable life. An easy life is a great danger for our union with Christ.

For all His followers, Our Lord asks that they deny themselves and take up their cross. Why that and for what purpose? Precisely to follow Our Divine Master, to imitate Him in all things and to become Christ-like. The example of Christ was an inspiration to many generous souls. Think of St. Francis of Assisi, the most perfect human copy of the Divine Model. Francis became Christ-like.

Think of Charles de Foucauld [1858-1916, beatified in 2005]. After his conversion, he considered himself the least of all, and out of great love for Christ gave up all pleasures, all comforts, and lived in greatest poverty, abnegations, and austerities. He has many followers everywhere in all nations, because he reflects Christ.

The lovers of the Crucified Lord, beginning with the Apostle St. Paul, were and are many. But also in our days, the love of money and pleasure has alienated many of our brothers and sisters from the Church and from God Himself.

There is certainly a healthy reaction in the world, especially among young people, against the materialistic and hedonistic culture. It is a reaction against immorality and pleasure. Some young men seek inspiration and guidance in the Oriental religions. Others, and they are not few, are coming back to Christ and are ready to give up everything: possessions, an earthly career, and many other things, in order to follow Christ, the Crucified and Risen Lord. Not a few of these young men will look in our direction and come and knock on our doors. They will look at us and observe our behavior. If they discover that we are not ready followers of Christ, that we love an easy and comfortable life, that we are earthly-minded, they will never enter. On the other hand, if the candidates see in us a sincere dedication to Christ the Crucified, sincere love of Christian poverty and Christian mortification, combined with a genuine and generous brotherly love, they will begin to think about joining us.

Here we see how important is the witness of our life. It is necessary that we have a deep spiritual life, rooted in Christ. We should be a living expression of the Gospel, a living witness of Christ Himself. Having that in mind, we can easily see how wrong are those who are practical enemies of the Cross, who dislike any mortification, any deprivation, but who are in search of comfort, of pleasure, of satisfaction, and an easy life. I hope no one of us is doing such things. But imagine a monastery, a religious house where the love for the Crucified Lord is gone and the spirit of the world has taken its place! Such houses cannot attract good vocations, and the bad ones will not persevere. May Our Lord preserve us from relaxation of observance, as we ask every evening after the Litany in our prayer.

If we have the spirit of Christ, if we are really His followers, with the grace of God and under the guidance of the Holy Spirit, we shall be able to discern what kind of modern conveniences, which practical achievements of our civilization and culture, we may use in our eremitical life, and to what extent we may use them. It would be difficult to make here an enumeration of all these things. But let us give some examples to understand better what I mean.

In the times of St. Benedict and St. Romuald, the monks used very simple tools for work. They dressed with the means of their times. They cooked as customary in their times. Of course they had no electricity, no refrigerators, or other such things which we have today.

Should we go back to the old style of life and take a negative attitude towards civilization? Are we permitted to use a car and, if necessary, an airplane, and still remain followers of Christ? Mother Teresa of Calcutta [1910-1997, beatified in 2003], the poorest of the poor, is often seen in airplanes, but always for Christ's sake. We see that a healthy discernment in this matter is necessary.

Next time we will continue further our reflections upon this theme.

Forgive me for dwelling so long on the same subject. Believe me, it is a vital question for all of us and for the future of this hermitage. On the one hand, we are living at the end of the 20th century. At our disposal are all the advantages of our modern civilization and culture. On the other hand, we are entirely dedicated to Christ and would like to follow His teaching and imitate His example as perfectly as possible. We should never betray Christ, but use technological advancements insofar as they are good and necessary, and also in harmony with our way of life. We must remain lovers of the Cross and of the Crucified, even if we make use of a typewriter, car, tractor, refrigerator, freezer, central heating, or modern laundry, and other things which seem necessary today. We should avoid, however, all exaggeration and self seeking, and remain men of great discretion, moderation, and mortification. Let us often ask ourselves: what would Christ do in our place?

As spiritual sons of St. Romuald and Bl. Paul Giustiniani, we also have a great responsibility to preserve the integrity of their eremitical charism in our times and for the future of the Church.

May our Crucified and Risen Lord bless us all. Amen.

9

SILENCE OF TOUCH (PART 3)

Today we shall finish our reflections on the sense of touch. We tried to see how we could bring to silence all the voices of our fallen nature, all unjustified, sinful, and harmful desires to satisfy our sensual tendencies which come from our sense of touch.

We have seen that discipline in our life is necessary. Very often we must say "no" to our bad tendencies. Very often we also must be able to say "yes," accepting crosses, accepting things disagreeable to our nature, but which are good for our soul. The austerities of our life will become very helpful in our personal and spiritual life. They will free us from sinful desires, they will help us to obtain perfect control, as far as it is possible; control, I repeat, over our bad inclinations, impulses, and tendencies. The austerities of our Christian life will help us to become free for God and for our Brothers, free for prayer, and unselfish love.

In the past, speaking about the mortification of our senses, I also mentioned the problem of hygiene. There is an old saying: "*Mens sana in corpore sano*," which is translated: "A sound mind in a sound body." Our body is given by God for a good purpose. We can abuse it in two ways: either by excess or by defect. By excess, we abuse our body and do harm to our soul. This happens as many times as we transgress the limits imposed by the commandments of God or by common sense, in seeking our own satisfaction. By defect, we abuse our body as many times as we refuse to give it what is necessary. To be able to pray and to work, we must also eat and rest. Sometimes it will be difficult to find the middle way between two extremes, between the "too much" and the "too little." There will often be a struggle in our life. More than once we shall have to ask ourselves: "Should I do it or should I abstain? Should I say 'yes,' or should I say 'no'?"

Some people will try to justify everything, and they never feel obliged to mortify themselves in anything. They rather think that all is permitted and justified before God. The Gospel teaches us something different.

Consider also, there could be excesses in denying all rights to the body. Some, for reason of mortification, put ashes in food, refuse to take a shower, or other things belonging to normal hygiene. We are told that St. Dominic Loricatus, one of the first generation Camaldolese, and very highly praised by St. Peter Damian himself, never took a bath and practiced the greatest austerities possible. He fasted, of course, flagellated himself almost unceasingly, reciting during this practice the Psalter. He [wore penitential] chains, and when he died, his body was found partly eaten by worms. I do not question the holiness of St. Dominic Loricatus, and I suppose he followed the inspirations of the Holy Spirit. His example, however, cannot be taken as a normal thing to be imitated — admired yes, imitated no!

A sound hygiene is necessary in our life. In our hermitage there is a shower in each cell. The daily use of the shower in the U.S.A. is a normal thing, especially during the period of great work and great heat. There is, however, no obligation to take a daily shower. Of course, we should wash ourselves everyday and keep clean. Also the laundry should be done regularly.

I remember when in Colombia, our candidates were very clean. They took a shower as much as three times a day. They used cold water, which is customary there.

What about our attitude toward pain and sickness? How should we behave? Are we permitted to use medicine to diminish our pain? Here we touch a very practical point. We have all had in the past and will have in the future some pain. It is a part of our human condition before we reach heaven.

Here, as everywhere, we should avoid extremes. Little things should be treated as such, and great things as being serious. How often, however, it happens that with the smallest inconvenience or pain, we behave as if we were inflicted with serious sickness. We imagine that we are really sick and become exigent and impatient. Let us not be concerned too much about our body. Let us follow the advice of a prudent doctor and that of our religious superior. There are imaginary sicknesses, which could become very dangerous because they can make psychological disturbances and become an obstacle in our spiritual progress. The devil will take advantage in such cases. He will suggest to us that we should lay down when it is time for work or prayer. He will tell us that we do not have enough vitamins or proteins in our organism, and many other things. Let us be attentive and not be afraid to accept crosses coming from God, nor be afraid to suffer a little.

We can also exaggerate virtue by not taking seriously real sickness. Of course, we must be mortified and ready to die. (Some give the impression that they prefer to stay on earth rather than to go to heaven!) But there could also be a lack of discretion, humility, and obedience.

Some refuse to go and see a doctor. Others refuse to take any medicine. Is that right or not? We cannot deny that many strong people have something heroic in them. They can endure many difficult things out of great love for God. How often, however, it happens that self-will, vanity, and other sentiments mingle in their souls. They are so full of themselves that they have no intention to submit to proper authority, or do what they are asked. Their pseudo-heroism is another form of pride and selfishness. Humility and obedience is more agreeable to God than exhibition of our strength.

No one is obliged to have recourse to extraordinary means to save his life, nor is there an obligation to prolong life artificially when the hour of death arrives. We should, however, treat our life as a gift from God and remain ready to fulfill our mission on earth to the end, accepting, if necessary, surgery, medications, and longer rest. Even a better diet could be in order to return to good health.

The last point: Do we have the right to take medicine when we have a pain in order to suffer less? If the medicine is not necessary but is only a tranquilizer, so to speak, I would say to try to do without it. But if you feel that you cannot fulfill your duties, or you become very impatient, bitter, uncharitable, then take the medicine, and remain a normal man. The same principle could be applied to other things: for instance, to fasting. If you can abstain from unnecessary food or practice a greater fast — do it. If, however, through fasting you would be unable to follow the regular life, to accomplish your duties, or if because of lack of food you would become angry, impatient, uncharitable — eat more and remain a normal man. With what I have said, I would not like to suppress fasting or mortification, but to practice these with discretion and moderation. There could still be said many things of a similar nature. I think, however, this should be enough for today.

We have finished our reflections on four of our five senses: our sight, our hearing, our taste, and our touch. We did not yet speak about the sense of smell. When we speak about it, it will be briefly.

I will finish with some quotations from the founder of the Opus Dei, Josemaria Escriva de Balaguer:

1. "Unless you mortify yourself, you'll never be a prayerful soul."
2. "Choose mortifications which don't mortify others."
3. "Where there is no mortification, there is no virtue."
4. "Interior mortification: I don't believe in your interior mortification if I see that you despise mortification of the senses — that you don't practice it."

May the Holy Spirit enlighten us and teach us how to mortify our senses and help us silence all other voices.

Amen.

10

SILENCE OF THE SENSE OF SMELL
AND THE INTERIOR SENSES

Today, we shall speak a few words about our sense of smell, and then go further in our reflections to the interior senses: memory and imagination.

The sense of smell, as with all other senses, is a gift from God, and should be used only for good purpose. Alas, it can also be abused and become an instrument leading to sins, even to great sins. Tanquerey, in *The Spiritual Life*, writes: "As to the sense of smell, suffice it to say that the immoderate use of perfumes is often but a pretext for satisfying sensuality, and at times a ruse to excite lust. Earnest Christians should use them with moderation; clerics and religious should never use them." I do not think that in our life colognes are used by anyone. But there is still room for mortification of our sense of smell — there are things which should be brought to silence.

I remember living in one community with a Brother who never ate fish because of the "bad smell of the fresh fish," as he said. I told him: "My Brother, you are running in the opposite direction. You should mortify your sense of smell and eat fish, which presents great advantages for your health." It was impossible to convince him or to remove his apprehension in this matter. The same Brother, however, liked the aroma of flowers on the altar.

Sometimes it happens that people are too sensitive and frequently seem to detect bad smells. They could become very disagreeable in the common life, and certainly should silence this tendency. I do not say that we should never use our sense of smell or that we should become insensible when we are in contact with the beauty and freshness of God's creation. For instance, while walking in the fields, or woods, and gardens, and a nice aroma of flowers comes to us, we should gratefully raise our soul to God, who in His goodness created all things for us. A good use of our senses is never an abuse.

Speaking about the sense of smell as a gift of God given for a good purpose, I would like to mention that many a danger can be detected by the sense of smell. The cook should also be attentive and see whether potatoes, onions, or other perishables are beginning to give a bad smell and to spoil.

Consider, many animals have a very acute sense of smell. It is almost unbelievable what they can detect and how far this sense can reach. This is a gift of God in lower creatures. I remember when in Colombia, about a hundred cows were grazing, day and night, on our property rented to a neighbor. When a cow died, many big birds, perhaps vultures, appeared shortly after and ate all that they could. How did the birds know that a cow was dead, and which one? Vultures are orientated by eyesight. In any case, the birds prevented a possible epidemic in the tropical climate. We all know how a cat can smell the mouse and vice versa. We know, also, how a dog, especially when trained, can sniff out drugs.

Let us finish this brief [reflection], giving thanks to God for the gift of smell, and let us also make the resolution to bring to silence the lack of mortification of our sense of smell.

Having finished our reflections upon the five external senses, we go a step higher to the internal senses: to our memory and imagination. Today we shall make a kind of introduction to our subject. I now quote Tanquerey: "The memory and imagination are two valuable faculties, which not only furnish the mind with the necessary material whereon to work, but enable it to explain the truth with the aid of images and facts in such a manner as to make it easier to grasp, and render it more vital and more interesting. The bare, colorless and cold statement of truth would not engage the interest of most men. It is not a question, then, of atrophying these faculties, but of schooling them, of subjecting their activity to the control of reason and will. Otherwise, left to themselves, they literally crowd the soul with a host of memories and images that distract the spirit, waste its energies, cause it to lose priceless time while at work or prayer, and constitute the source of a thousand temptations against purity, charity, humility and other virtues. Hence, of necessity they must be disciplined and made to minister to the higher faculties of the soul." (p. 376)

The same author continues: "In order to check the wanderings of the memory and the imagination, we must, first of all strive to expel from the outset, that is, from the very moment we are aware of them, all dangerous fancies and recollections. Furthermore, since frequent daydreaming by a kind of psychological necessity leads us into dangerous musings, we should take heed to provide against idle thought, by mortifying ourselves as regards useless fancies, which constitute a waste of time and pave the way to others of an even more perilous nature. The best means to attain this end is to apply ourselves wholeheartedly to the performance of the duties of the moment, to our work, to our studies, to our ordinary occupations."

Tanquerey makes also the following observation: "Let young men remember that in order to succeed, either in studies or in their profession, they must give more play to the mind and the will than to the lower faculties. Thus, whilst making provision for the future, they should avoid all dangerous flights of the imagination." (p. 377)

Tanquerey continues: "Lastly, the memory and the imagination will prove most helpful if they are employed to nourish our piety, by searching in Scriptures, in the Liturgy, and in spiritual writers the choicest texts, the most beautiful similes, the richest imagery, and if the imagination is used to enter into God's presence, to picture in their details the mysteries of Our Lord and the Blessed Virgin. Thus, far from stunting this faculty, we shall fill it with devout representations which will displace dangerous fancies and enable us the better to grasp and present to our hearers the beauty of the Gospel scenes." So much for Tanquerey at the moment.

The next time we shall go more into detail and practical applications. Let us remember, however, that our memory and our imagination should be in the service of our intellectual faculties, of our mind and our will. They become harmful for our spiritual life, even for normal human life, when they become leaders and masters. The memory and the imagination should become a help in our spiritual life, not an obstacle. When they have the tendency to become an obstacle, they must be brought to silence.

Bless us, Mary Maiden mild,
Bless us too, her tender Child.
Amen.

11

Silence of the Memory

Last Saturday, we made a general introduction to our reflections on our interior senses: our memory and our imagination. Today we shall go into more detail, beginning with our memory. We shall underline the good qualities of our memory, but we shall also study the dangers and obstacles which can come from an unmortified memory.

Our internal senses, as well as the external ones, are a gift from God given for good purpose. We could ask ourselves: What is the purpose of our memory? Why did God give us memory? Generally speaking, we received the memory to remember what we have heard and seen. But as Father [Jordan] Aumann, O.P., writes in his book, *Spiritual Theology*, "We make a distinction between the sense memory which has for its object only the sensible, the particular and the concrete, and the intellectual memory which deals with the suprasensible, the abstract, and the universal."

"The memory can give inestimable service to the intellect and can be its most powerful ally. Without it, our spirit would be like a sieve that is always empty, however much water is poured into it. For certain types of knowledge, such as languages, history, the physical and material sciences, an excellent memory is indispensable," says Fr. Aumann.

Some people have a phenomenal memory. Consider a pianist, a real artist who plays for many hours the most difficult compositions and never looks at the notes. Usually he does not have any notes before his eyes. He plays all from memory.

Consider another who knows a book of Holy Scripture, or quotes from other books by heart. Take people who remember word for word a sermon, a conversation, or other things they have heard.

We can imagine the first disciples of Christ, how they conserved in their memory what they had heard, and transmitted all to their children, to friends, to new converts. Of course, there often was a special intervention of the Holy Spirit in these persons.

Take another example: how often children remember with veneration and gratitude the recommendations of their good parents. How often religious and priests remember what they heard during the years of their formation and continue to make good use of it. There are many, many good things which the memory conserves for a long time, even forever.

Alas, there are also evil things stored in the human memory. Thus, begins the problem. Father Aumann writes: "Throughout life we experience many things that are of no use whatever for the sanctification of the soul. Many of them destroy the soul's peace and tranquility which are so necessary for a life of prayer and recollection."

Yes, indeed, many of our reminiscences can become harmful, and therefore they should be silenced.

Father Aumann gives four practical recommendations, in this matter:

1. Forget past sins.
2. Cease thinking of past injuries.
3. Remember benefits from God.
4. Consider motives for Christian hope.

1. The first step is to forget past sins. That is absolutely necessary for all who aspire to eternal salvation. "The remembrance of one's own sins or those of another," says Fr. Aumann, "has a strong power for suggesting to the soul the same things by way of a new temptation, and of disposing it to sin again, especially when a vivid imagination

is associated with the recollection. The soul must immediately and energetically reject any remembrance of this kind."

Here we could add that in many cases the memory conserves also useless things. It becomes a storage of rubbish, of intellectual garbage, and other things. In this case a purification is necessary. Everything should be brought to silence, especially if our ideal is purity of heart and Christian perfection.

2. Cease thinking about past injuries, recommends Father Aumann. This pertains to virtue and is indispensable for any soul that wishes to sanctify itself. Many, however, have difficulties in forgetting received injuries. They forgive, but do not forget. In spite of a pardon that has been given, the remembrance of a past offence will disturb the peace of conscience and present the guilty party in an unfavorable light. One should forget the disagreeable episode and realize that our offences against God are much greater, and that He demands that we pardon others in order to receive pardon. Father Aumann concludes: "The soul that nourishes rancor, however justifiable it may seem (and it never is in the eyes of God), can forget about reaching sanctity."

3. Remember benefits received from God, recommends Fr. Aumann in his *Spiritual Theology*. The recollection of the immense benefits we have received from God, of the times He has pardoned our faults, of the dangers from which He has preserved us, of the loving care He has exercised over us, is an excellent means of arousing our gratitude toward Him and the desire of corresponding more faithfully with His graces. And if to this we add the remembrance of our disobedience and rebellion, of our ingratitude and resistance to grace, our soul will be filled with humility and confusion and will experience the need of redoubling its vigilance and its efforts to be better in the future. As we can see, we should not remember our past sins with all their details, still less nourish with this remembrance our imagination and expose ourselves to new temptations or new sins. But we should have a deep interior compunction for all sins we ever committed. It would not be an exaggeration to say that we will grow in the spiritual life in proportion to our compunction of heart. We pray in Psalm 50, "A humbled, contrite heart you will not spurn."

4. Speaking about memory, Father Aumann invites us to consider motives for Christian hope. It is one of the most efficacious means for directing our memory to God and for purifying it of contact with earthly things. St. John of the Cross makes the memory the seat of Christian hope and shows how growth in this virtue effectively purges the memory. The remembrance of an eternity of happiness, which is the central object of Christian hope, is most apt for making us disdain the things of earth and causing us to raise our spirits to God.

In conclusion of what has been said today, I would like to repeat that our memory is a precious gift from God and should serve for a good purpose. It should help us to become good Christians and to grow in the spiritual life. If our memory does not help us to come closer to God, but rather makes it more difficult, our memory needs purification. Many things should be brought to absolute silence. There exists an active and a passive purification of our senses and our spirit. God has His own ways to purify our senses and our mind. He permits dryness and deprives us of all consolation. He permits great temptations against faith, hope, and charity; also, against patience and peace of soul. Little by little, we become detached from ourselves and from earthly pleasures, and come closer to God and are ready for higher contemplation. Please God that we may be strong, generous, and patient during God's work of purification in ourselves. Please God that we enjoy, with His help, perfect silence in all our senses, both internal and external, but also in our intellectual faculties. Bring to silence all that is not from God or conducive to God. Then we will be ready for greater union with Christ, for greater contemplation and love of God.

Amen.

12

SILENCE OF THE IMAGINATION

Today, we shall speak about the silence to be imposed on our imagination.

As we have seen in previous conferences, all senses and faculties received from God are good, but can be abused in many ways. Also, our imagination is given for a good purpose and should help us in our spiritual life. The imagination, when under control of higher faculties, inspired by faith, can be a great help in meditating on the meaning of revealed truths. Tanquerey says the "colorless and cold statement of truth would not engage the interest of most men." [Quoted above in Conference 10, p. 42-43]

Our Lord frequently made use of the imagination to place the great mysteries within the grasp of the people by means of beautiful parables and allegories. The imagination has also great influence over the sensitive appetite and is a help for our intellect. Fr. Chaignon [Peter Chaignon, S.J.] in an introduction to meditation says: "By the imagination an object is rendered present to us; we see it, so to speak, hear it, touch it, taste it... Now, to apply this faculty and our senses to some truth of faith, as far as this truth is susceptible of such application, or to some mystery of Our Lord Jesus Christ, is to make what is called application of the senses. This exercise consists, then, in this, that the soul by means of the imagination, conceives itself to hear words, to touch objects," etc. The same author continues: "This process will be quite the opposite if there is question of a vice."

As we know, the remembrance of our past sins, recalled with all details and helped by our imagination, can become a new temptation and a great danger of committing new sins. For this reason, when meditating upon vices, we should be careful not to fall into this trap.

Later on, as we progress in our spiritual life, the imagination should be held more and more under the control of our intellectual faculties animated by faith. Indeed, there could be for some souls a great danger of pseudo-visions and pseudo-apparitions produced by the imagination and deep emotions. The devil knows how to make good profit in such cases.

The Cistercian Abbot [Vital] Lehodey, in his book, *The Ways of Mental Prayer*, writes: "Even canonized Saints have not always been able to avoid the deceits of the demon or the reveries of the imagination." Father Lehodey continues: "Who does not know how urgently St. John of the Cross exhorts his readers to distrust visions, revelations or locutions, to resist them, and to get rid of them." St. Teresa gives her readers the same counsel. "In such matters," she writes, "there is always reason to fear, until the soul is certain that they proceed from the Spirit of God. This is why I say that, in the beginning, the best course to adopt is always to combat them. If God is their author, this humility of the soul in guarding herself against such favors will only the better dispose her for receiving them, and the more she puts them to the test, the more they will increase." (*Interior Castle*, 6th mans. c. 3) St. Teresa, when speaking of Our Lord's apparitions, adds: "Never ask Him, never even wish Him to lead you by this way. This way is, no doubt, good, and you ought to hold it in high esteem and respect, but it is unseemly either to ask or to desire it." (Ibid., c. 9)

To conclude this point, I would like to mention how prudent and relatively slow the Church is in approving private revelations and apparitions. Normally, all the phenomena are tested, studied, and finally discerned and declared as coming from God or not. In recent years we have had many pseudo revelations and apparitions which the Church did not approve. I will cite two cases in which the supposed apparitions of Our Lady were not approved by the authority of the Church — at Garabandal (Spain) and in the diocese of Brescia (Italy).

More examples could be given which confirm what was said by St. Teresa and St. John of the Cross on the matter of resisting visions, apparitions, and locutions — they may not be from God.

There are many other dangers which could arise if we do not control our imagination. Father Aumann, O.P., says "There is nothing that can cause greater difficulty on the way to sanctification than an imagination that has broken away from the control of reason enlightened by faith."

Father Aumann, in *Spiritual Theology*, continues: "There are two principal obstacles caused by an uncontrolled imagination: dissipation and temptation. Without recollection, an interior life and a life of prayer are impossible, and there is nothing that so impedes recollection as the inconstancy and dissipation of the imagination. Freed of any restraint, it paints in vivid colors the pleasure sin provides for the concupiscible appetite or exaggerates the difficulty the irascible appetite will encounter on the road to virtue, thus leading to discouragement. But the difficulties can be avoided if we use the proper means."

Fr. Aumann enumerates four means to avoid the above-mentioned dangers of seeking illicit pleasure and of discouragement. What are these beneficial means?

1. Custody of the External Senses
2. Prudent Selection of Reading Matter
3. Attention to the Duty of the Moment
4. Indifference to Distractions

1. Custody of the External Senses

We spoke already of the custody of the external senses and of the necessity of bringing to silence all that could become a danger or an obstacle to our spiritual life. Fr. Aumann says: "It is necessary to control the external senses, and especially the sense of sight, because they provide the images the imagination retains, reproduces, and reassembles, thus arousing the passions and encouraging the consent of the will. There is no better way to avoid temptations from this source than to deprive the imagination of such images by custody of the external senses."

2. Prudent Selection of Reading Matter

I shall continue to quote Fr. Aumann: "It is not only a question of reading matter that is evil or obviously dangerous, but also that which fills the imagination with useless images. There are occasions when it is beneficial to engage in light reading for relaxation. It is, in fact, a good practice to relieve tension or to rest one's mental powers in this way. But it is likewise necessary to provide holy and profitable material so that the imagination will be directed positively to the good. This is where spiritual reading can contribute a great deal to the proper use of the imagination."

I would like to make a personal observation. It is of great importance that we have good books for our spiritual reading. We can find them in our library. But let us avoid two dangers — curiosity and mental indigestion. Curiosity can go so far so that we do not observe our schedule; for instance, retiring very late in the evening. Thereby, we expose ourselves to dissipation, distractions, and temptations, thus creating great obstacles for our life of prayer. On the other hand, there will be a danger of looking always for new books, of not finishing the first, especially when we are in difficulties, or when we do not have spiritual consolation. I saw a novice bring back to the library more then fifty books one day in a wheelbarrow. Uncontrolled and unmortified reading can cause confusion and spiritual indigestion. Who has the greatest profit in such cases? — certainly the devil! The evil one can easily approach a soul which is restless, fearful, living in anxiety, and in search of consolation. Let us be on our guard and use discretion and patience while reading.

3. Attention to the Duty of the Moment

Fr. Aumann gives us a third means to avoid dangers coming from an uncontrolled imagination. He says: "The habit of attending to the duty of the moment has the double advantage of concentrating our intellectual powers and of disciplining the imagination by preventing it from being distracted to other objects. It also helps a person avoid idleness, which is one of the primary sources of dissipation."

4. Indifference to Distractions

Finally, we should be indifferent to distractions. What does that mean? Fr. Aumann explains: "There is no sure way of avoiding all distractions, but one can always ignore them. Indeed, this is a much more effective measure than to combat them directly." One should take no account of them, but should do what must be done in spite of an uncontrolled imagination. It is possible to keep one's mind and heart fixed on God even in the midst of involuntary distractions.

In conclusion, we should both use our imagination as long as it helps us in our spiritual life, and keep it under the strict control of our higher faculties enlightened by faith. The custody of our external senses, a prudent selection of our reading matter, the attention to our present duty, and indifference to distractions will help us to avoid dangers and to remove obstacles in our life of recollection and prayer.

May All Saints, whose Solemnity we celebrate tomorrow, help us to follow their good examples and to reach safely our eternal destination.

Amen.

13

SILENCE OF THE INTELLECTUAL FACULTIES

Having spoken about the silence to be imposed on our external and internal senses, we come today to the intellectual faculties.

As we know, man was created in the image of God. We read in Genesis (1:26-27): "God said: Let us make man in our image, in the likeness of ourselves, and let them be masters of the fish of the sea, the birds of heaven, the cattle, all the wild beasts and all the reptiles that crawl upon the earth. God created man in the image of himself, in the image of God he created him, male and female he created them."

As we can see, man is the crown of all creatures. He is their master. For that reason, we share with God and the heavenly court the use of the intellectual faculties. We received even more than that: man was elevated by God to the supernatural order. The Catholic Faith teaches us that our first parents, before the Fall, were endowed with sanctifying grace. After their Fall, Christ came to redeem us and to restore us to the state of sanctifying grace. Through the Sacrament of Baptism we become a new creation, adopted sons of God. Our spiritual life is nourished and renewed by the grace of God, especially by the use of the Sacraments, which Christ has given to His Church.

Man has something in common with all creatures, but also with the Creator. Through our body and senses we have something in common with all creatures on earth, from the lowest to the highest. We have also something in common with the angels and God

Himself, but in a far different degree; we have an immortal soul with intellectual faculties. Fr. Aumann says: "According to traditional psychology, there are two spiritual faculties of the soul: the intellect and the will. Some mystical authors, including St. John of the Cross, considered the intellectual memory as a faculty distinct from the intellect and the will, but modern psychology classifies it as a function of the intellect; consequently, we should speak of the two spiritual faculties that are really distinct: the intellect and the will."

The intellect is the spiritual faculty by which we apprehend things in an immaterial way. The senses are the way to the intellect. Following a Thomistic axiom, based on the Greek philosopher Aristotle, *"nihil in intellectu quod non praevius aliquomodo in sensu."* (Nothing is in the intellect which did not come in some way through the senses.) Once more, we can see how important is both the control and the mortification of our senses. If we become masters of our external and internal senses, then our intellectual faculties and our spiritual life will become free from many obstacles, but also free for revealed Truth, for Christ, for God.

The intellect provides cognitive knowledge, but it has also the faculty to pronounce judgments. It occurs when the intellect compares two ideas. Normally it affirms or denies the connection between them. We can also abstain from judgment. This is necessary when we are inclined to make a rash judgment, or an unjust and uncharitable one.

The human intellect is not free from the danger of error. It can occur through lack of attention and concentration. It can also happen through ignorance. Finally, it very often comes from the refusal of our mind to accept the truth. Consequently, a favorable disposition in ourselves is necessary. There is a need for recollection. Dissipation is our enemy and an obstacle for our intellect to function properly. We should act with great concentration of mind, taking all the necessary time to come to true knowledge or to form right judgment. Serious study should not be neglected in order to avoid ignorance of things which we should know. Finally, all *"parti pris,"* as the Frenchmen say, all prejudices or preconceived judgments or opinions, must disappear if the intellect is to function normally. Many opinionated men, unduly attached to their own opinion, will have a hard time changing their erroneous ideas. We must tolerate and accept others as they are and love them sincerely as Christ is asking us to do. The same refers to the acceptance of and submission to the Magisterium of the Church. Another danger for our intellect, apart from error and prejudices, is the attitude of pure intellectual curiosity which engages in the study of sacred truths as a purely scholastic pursuit, instead of seeing them as truths by which one lives. Also, Lucifer indeed knows very much about God and theology, even more than we all together, but he does not live accordingly — he has no love, he even hates God and us.

The intellect is a great gift from God, but we can use it in two directions: We can come closer to God and become Christ-like, or resemble more and more Lucifer and the fallen angels.

Intellectual deviations can go in various directions: for instance, reading things without value for our spiritual life (thus multiplying and aggravating the intellectual rubbish in our soul); or studying for the sake of vainglory and of imaginary greatness, and by doing so, giving to the devil the keys to the interior castle, the soul. Intellectual pride hinders the action of the Holy Spirit in us. Indeed, God resists the proud, as Holy Scripture teaches us, and He gives His graces to the humble.

A great intellect is a great gift from God, but it does not exist without great dangers. All heresiarchs, or leaders in heresy, have been gifted men. So also in our days, the great troublemakers within the Church, whether on the traditional side or on the progressive one, are not submissive to the Church's Magisterium.

For all of us who aspire towards a deeper spiritual life and are in search for a greater union with God, it is a duty, a great obligation, to bring to silence our exaggerated intellectual curiosity and our imaginary greatness. It is also our duty to avoid rash and uncharitable judgments. We must become free from all obstacles which impede us to accept the truth, especially revealed truth, and to live accordingly. The soul must let itself be led by the light of faith, which is the proximate and proportionate means for the union of the intellect with God in this life. St. John of the Cross, in his *Ascent of Mount Carmel*, writes: "The greater the faith of the soul, the more closely is it united with God." Scupoli, the author of the *Spiritual Combat*, writes: "This is the pride that renders faith and obedience to superiors difficult. One wants to be self-sufficient; the more confidence one has in one's own judgment the more reluctantly does one accept the teachings of faith, or the more readily does one submit these to criticism and to personal interpretation." Tanquerey gives us some practical advice as to how to overcome intellectual pride. First of all, we must submit ourselves with child-like docility to the teachings of faith. Further on, in the discussions we hold with others, we must seek not the satisfaction of our pride and the triumph of our ideas, but the truth. The best means of drawing close to the truth, as well as observing the laws of humility and charity, is to listen attentively and without prejudice to the reasons adduced by our opponents and to admit whatever is true in their remarks.

St. Augustine calls those who cause unfortunate dissensions dividers of unity, enemies of peace, without charity, puffed up with vanity, well pleased with themselves, and great in their own eyes.

May the Holy Spirit enlighten us in order to understand better how we should make good use of our intellect on our way to deeper union with God. May He teach us also how to become docile, humble, and obedient to God and His representatives on earth. Finally, may the Holy Spirit, the Personified love of God, teach us how to love the truth and how to love those who have different ideas than our own.

At the beginning of our conference I quoted from Genesis the account of the creation of man. As we remember, God said: "Let us make man in our own image, in the likeness of ourselves." (Gen 1:26) Yes, we were created in God's image and we were reborn through Baptism. But as some of the Greek Fathers put it: Our duty, our goal during all our life is to render our likeness to God more and more perfect. To become more God-like or Christ-like, we should on the one hand avoid all sin and combat vices, but on the other hand, we should acquire virtues, especially perfect love. Only God can make us God-like, but He needs our faithful and generous cooperation. He gave us intellectual faculties, especially free will, and, consequently, He cannot save us without our humble, docile, and obedient "Yes."

The next time we shall speak about our free will.

O Holy Spirit, Kindle with fire from above,
each sense, and fill our hearts with love;
Grant to our flesh, so weak and frail,
That strength of Thine which cannot fail.

Amen.

14

SILENCE OF THE WILL (PART 1)

Today we shall speak about our free will and about submitting ourselves to the will of God. Let us not be afraid or think that we shall lose our personality, or lose something which we hold in high esteem. In reality, what we give up is not so important as that which we receive in exchange. We give up our disorder and imperfection in order to grow spiritually, and even psychologically, as free persons and children of God.

Now let us speak about our free will, our greatest gift on the natural level. God wanted that we decide ourselves about our future life and about many other things. The free choice, the free decision is what counts in the eyes of God. God does not like it when men behave as "robots" or voluntary slaves. We are created in the image and likeness of God and must make good use of our intellect and our free will.

The will, also called the rational appetite, is the faculty by which we seek the good as known by the intellect. It is distinguished from the sensitive appetite, which instinctively seeks the good as known by the senses. Even animals possess a sensitive appetite, but the rational appetite is proper to intellectual beings. The proper object of the will is the good proposed to it by the intellect, but in the appreciation or evaluation of the good, error may creep in. The intellect can judge as true good something which is only an apparent good. The will, which is a blind faculty, and always follows the apprehension of the intellect, will be impelled toward that object which is taken as if it were a true good.

When we hear that someone has committed suicide, we can be sure that the poor man thought that suicide would be a liberation from some greater difficulties. He thinks that the momentary suffering of killing himself would be a lesser suffering than the suffering he was experiencing. Of course, people who commit suicide do not think about punishment in eternity. Very often they lack deeper faith and are psychologically irresponsible.

The principle that the object of the will is the good proposed to it is always valid — even when one erroneously takes for a good what really is not a good, especially not for the soul. The proper act of the will is love, or the effective union of the will with a known good. All the movements or partial aspects of the human acts that take place in the will, such as simple volition, efficacious tendencies, consent, active use of the faculties, and fruition, proceed from love, directly or indirectly.

Father Aumann, in his *Spiritual Theology*, says that love can be divided in many ways. By reason of the object, love can be sensual or spiritual. By reason of modality, love can be natural or supernatural. By reason of the formal object or motive, love can be a love of concupiscence or of benevolence.

It is called a love of concupiscence when one desires the good insofar as it is good for oneself (egoistic motive); it is a love of benevolence if one loves another precisely insofar as the other is good and lovable; it is a love of friendship if the love is directed to a person and is a mutual and benevolent love.

Fr. Aumann gives some examples. He says "The sensual person loves with a love of concupiscence the object that gives pleasure; the blessed in heaven habitually love God with a love of benevolence, taking complacence in His infinite perfection and rejoicing that God is infinitely happy in Himself." Fr. Aumann says also that "The blessed in heaven and the people sanctified by grace here on earth love God with the love of friendship under the impulse of the virtue of charity."

We can add that acts of the will may be elicited or impetrated. They are called elicited if they proceed directly from the will (for instance — to consent, to choose, to love). They are called impetrated (commanded) acts when they are performed by some other faculty under the command of the will (for instance — when the will commands to study, to work, to mortify oneself voluntarily, etc.).

In our present situation we should be aware that human nature and all its faculties are profoundly affected by original sin. Consequently, once the orientation to God has been weakened, the will itself is readily inclined to selfishness.

Therefore, in our present situation the will must be corrected by a double effort. First of all, our effort should go towards total submission of our will to God and to conformity to His divine will. Secondly, a great effort is necessary to increase the power of the will with regard to the interior faculties until it can subject them completely to itself. In other words, one must attempt to regain, at the cost of great effort and the help of grace, the initial rectitude that the will enjoyed when it came forth from the creative hands of God.

In our 13 preceding conferences we tried to bring order to our interior faculties and to our intellect itself. We spoke about our external senses, which are, as it were, five doors leading to our soul. We spoke of the memory and our imagination, the interior senses, which can be a help to our intellect but can also become a great obstacle. All the mentioned faculties must be brought to the right order. A silence should be imposed on deviations and care should be taken that they do not become a hindrance or an obstacle in our spiritual life. Our intellect also must submit to Christian ascesis and discipline. It must be illuminated by faith. Let us also remember that from our intellect to our will, a long road is often the division. A Latin poet — Ovid — expressed what I am saying in the following verse: "*Video meliora, proboque, deteriora sequor.*" It means: I see better things and approve them, but I follow the less good ones (or the worst, if you wish).

The next time we shall come back to the same subject. Let us finish our present conference with two thoughts, one from St. Thomas Aquinas and one from St. Augustine.

St. Thomas says that egoism or disordered self-love is the origin and root of all sin. St. Augustine says: "Two loves have erected two cities; self-love, carried to the extreme of disdain of God, has built the city of the world; the love of God, carried to the point of disdain for one's self, has constructed the city of God. The one glories in itself, the other glories in the Lord."

My Brothers, we received the precious gifts of deep faith and of freedom. Let us make the right choice with all consequences in time and for eternity. Amen.

15

Silence of the Will (part 2)

L ast Saturday we spoke about our free will and the necessity to submit it to the will of God. We spoke also about the necessity of increasing the power of the will with regard to the inferior faculties until it can subject them completely to itself. Today we shall continue our meditation upon the same subject.

"We should remember and it should become evident," says Fr. Aumann, "that we cannot achieve total submission of our will to God unless we first detach ourselves from excessive love of created things; from the self-centered love of created things and from the self-centered love that runs counter to the demands of charity."

It is helpful to know that St. John of the Cross reduces his whole spiritual doctrine to this detachment from creatures as the negative element, and to union with God through love as the positive element. "It is a fact," says Fr. Aumann, "that the soul is filled with God in the measure and to the degree that it empties itself of creatures — and, of course, of self-centered love." Fr. Aumann is very clear on this point: "Detachment from created things is absolutely indispensable for arriving at Christian perfection," he says, "but it would be of little avail to detach oneself from external things if one is not likewise detached from one's own ego which constitutes the greatest of all obstacles to one's free flight to God." St. Thomas — as we said last Saturday — states that egoism or disordered self-love is the origin and root of all sin.

Let us pause a little and reflect upon this important point. Detachment from all creatures is indispensable, we heard, to reach perfection. But it is not enough. It would even be of little avail to detach oneself from external things if we are not detached from ourselves, from our self-love and self-will. Here is a stumbling block for many candidates who aspire to the monastic life in general and to our life in particular.

Detachment from creatures and detachment from ourselves, which never was easy in the past, will in the future present even greater difficulties for young candidates. A deep faith is necessary to understand that creatures can become a great obstacle to our union with God, and that we are our own greatest enemy because of our exaggerated self-esteem and self-love.

We have seen that for many new candidates self-denial and obedience seem an unacceptable condition for their spiritual growth. They will not believe that a deeper conversion is necessary to enter and to grow in the monastic life. Even the best candidates can have a hard time accepting without reluctance and without tears what we call detachment from creatures and detachment from ourselves. We can see by experience that modern psychology and revealed faith do not always exist together in harmony. As an example, take the existence of original sin and its consequences for all men. If we have deep faith we accept the fact that our human nature and all its faculties were profoundly affected by original sin. We also accept the necessity of a double effort, namely, to subject our will to God by total submission and to put order in our inferior faculties. Total submission to God will be possible only if we agree to detach ourselves from exaggerated love for creatures and ourselves.

Let us hope that in due time and with the grace of God, all who are called by our Lord to this form of life which is ours, will understand and accept what God is asking from them — even to great sacrifices. I mentioned that the younger generation has a hard time understanding and accepting things which seem unacceptable or difficult. But we must also try to understand the point of view of young people and be patient with them. They usually have good will, but are faced with too many obstacles to change their mind, their heart, and their life. Very often they try to defend themselves and react against the past. That seems to be a normal phenomenon, which has always existed. What is new, however, is the degree or the extent of their attitudes and reactions.

To understand our youth, we must keep in mind that on the one hand we live in an age of opulence, of material goods and pleasures. On the other hand, we are witnesses of a spiritual and moral decline. I will give some characteristic symptoms of the decline of our modern culture. In many countries more money is spent for killing than for helping or saving life. The race for new and more powerful arms becomes a great paradox. Legalized abortion and the public money given for the purpose of killing unborn babies is certainly a sign of mental aberration and of moral decline. Even the phenomenon of not desiring children is in itself abnormal and a sign of deep moral crises. There are many other symptoms of moral decline, such as official lies, violence, unfaithfulness to given promises and commitments. There can be no doubt that divorce and laicization of priests and religious have a great influence upon our youth. Consequently, they try to defend themselves, their futures, and their lives.

We could add other reasons that young people behave and react as they do. But we can be sure that many of them, with the grace of God, will look as to how they can live better lives and become better men, better Christians. I am sure that in the near future, many young people will come to our hermitages and, after the first difficulties of adjustment, will accept our life and will find the way to real happiness and holiness.

I shall finish for today with two quotations from Escriva de Balaguer's *The Way*: "Let obstacles only make you bigger. The grace of Our Lord will not be lacking. Through the very midst of the mountains the water shall pass. You will pass through mountains!"

"What does it matter that you have to curtail your activity for the moment, if later, like a spring which has been compressed, you'll advance much farther than you ever dreamed."

May God bless us in our efforts.

Amen.

16

SILENCE OF SELF-ESTEEM (PART 1)

We are still reflecting on how to bring our own will to silence in order to follow the will of God, which leads us to real holiness and happiness.

We have seen how important it is for our spiritual growth and for our eternal salvation to give up what does not lead to God. We should become detached from creatures and from ourselves. Detached from ourselves means from exaggerated self-esteem and self-love which is manifested by our own will.

It would be a disaster if people living in common in religious life were not inclined to give up their own will, nor to submit to the will of God as manifested by holy obedience.

Usually, people attached to their own views will also have the tendency to impose upon others their will, their likes and dislikes, their whims and other manifestations of their imperfection and immaturity. If a house of God is not animated by total submission to God through holy obedience, it will not become a house of peace, of love and happiness. Rather, it will be a place of unrest and disorder, of envy and hate. It will not be a house of prayer, or a witness to the kingdom of God, but rather an object of scandal.

Fr. Aumann writes in his *Spiritual Theology*: "The soul that aspires to perfect union with God must strive energetically against its own self-love, which subtly penetrates even holy things. It must examine the true motive for its actions, continually rectify its intentions, and not place as its goal or as the good of all its activities and efforts anything other than the glory of God and the perfect fulfillment of His divine will. It must keep constantly in mind the decisive words of Christ Himself, who makes perfect self-abnegation the indispensable condition for following Him: 'Whoever wishes to be my follower must deny his very self, take up his cross each day, and follow in my steps.'" (Lk 9:23)

As we remember, St. Thomas Aquinas said that disordered self-love is the origin and root of all sin. Fr. Aumann makes a practical comment: "Because it is the root of all sins, the manifestations of self-love are varied and almost infinite." So far as it affects spiritual things, self-love becomes the center around which everything else must rotate. Some persons seek themselves in everything, even in holy things: in prayer, which they prolong when they find sweetness and consolation in it, but which they abandon when they experience aridity; in the reception of the sacraments, which they seek only for sensible consolation; in spiritual direction, which they consider a note of distinction and in which, therefore, they always seek the director who is most popular, or who will let them live in peace with their egoistic values and selfish aims; in the very desire for sanctification, which they do not subordinate to the glory of God and the good of souls, but which they direct to themselves as the best ornament of their souls here on earth and as the source of increased happiness and glory in heaven. We would never finish if we were to attempt to list the manifestations of excessive self-love!"

When we recited Psalm 118 at Terce last Thursday, I was deeply impressed by the following words: "Your will is my heritage for ever, the joy of my heart!" (Psalm 118[119]: 111)

Here we see an ideal for ourselves. The will of God is our heritage for ever and the joy of our heart.

I will be quite open. When I began the religious life fifty years ago, I had quite different convictions and attitudes in my spiritual life than I have today. I will not deny that I was idealistic and not free from selfishness. It is commonly thought that young people are often too idealistic and not realistic enough; also, that young people have a tendency to dream, know too much, and prematurely think they are quite advanced in the spiritual life. Some years ago I reminded a candidate for our life that he was only a beginner. He replied: "I am not a beginner, I have behind me seven years of Transcendental Meditation." He was twenty-four years old.

Well, after fifty years of religious life, I still feel as though I am a beginner, one very far from perfection. I feel really truthful in my soul when I pray with the publican of the Gospel, "God, be merciful to me, a sinner." (Lk 18:14)

Yes, there was a time long ago, when I thought I was becoming more and more sinless. I even nourished a false ideal that to be without sin would automatically make me holy. A great illusion! It reminds me of what Bossuet said to the Cistercian nuns at Port-Royal, which became a stronghold of the heresy of Jansenism: "You are chaste as angels, but proud as demons." Indeed there exists a danger for all of us of becoming proud of our achievements in the spiritual life. Intellectual pride and spiritual pride can kill or gravely impede the best beginnings of a life for God. We know well that God resists any form of pride, and only to the humble does He give His graces. Christ came to seek the lost sheep, the Prodigal son. In one word, He came to save sinners. If we recognize that we really are sinners, we will then become more open and docile to the action of the Holy Spirit, and He will sanctify us and make us Christ-like, that is, holy.

If someone had told me fifty or even forty years ago that there was much self-love and self-will in me, even in spiritual things, I would have been very astonished. In my own thought I felt I was more perfect, or closer to God, than I was in reality. During my life I have given up many wrong attitudes and ideas. But more so, I have seen my imperfections, my limitations, and my nothingness. What is amazing over the years is that the more I have seen my sinfulness and needs, the more joyful and confident in God I have become. Our retreat master, in his last conference, explained very well how important it is to die to ourselves, to make room for Christ in our soul and in our whole personality.

The next time we shall see what the Desert Fathers and St.

Benedict taught about self-love and self-will. In the meantime we should continue to co-operate with the Holy Spirit, the Sanctifier of our souls, who was given to us by our Heavenly Father and our Lord Jesus Christ in order to help us become adoptive children of God and to behave as true children of God.

The secret of our spiritual growth is full confidence in God and filial love. Then, prayer and mortification will not present any problem. Doing that, we shall wholeheartedly agree with the Psalmist that the will of God is our heritage for ever and the joy of our heart.

Amen.

17

Silence of Self-Esteem (part 2)

We are still meditating on how we can better control our own will and self-love in order to become totally free to submit to God and to do His Holy Will. Of course, there is no question of becoming a "robot" who makes mechanical movements, or one who keeps observances and customs only externally. Rather, we are looking at how we can submit to God with all our heart and fulfill His Holy Will out of sincere and perfect love. Freedom and love are two great gifts we receive from God and we should keep them intact and develop them as perfectly as possible.

Every act which we perform in our spiritual life, as well as on a human level, or in community, should be a free gift from ourselves and animated by great Christian love, embracing both love of God and love of neighbor. If an act is not freely performed, but done under constraint or out of great fear, such an act has no value at all, or little value, depending on the degree of freedom still left and the good intention. An act performed without love is an external act lacking the most perfect quality.

What we are expected to do is to perform all our duties out of personal conviction and free choice animated by supernatural love. We should strive during all our life to become both free from ourselves and free for God. Exaggerated self-love and self-will are great impediments on our way to perfection, to become really free for God. When our passions and emotions arise and disturb our spiritual balance, pushing us into illicit desires and actions, or making us more obstinate in our exaggerated self-esteem and self-will, we risk becoming slaves and victims of our weaknesses, and we are not free enough for God.

The more we become free from self, the better we are. Normally, we must go through great struggles and do violence to ourselves in order to become free from our weaknesses and sins, but also, what is more important — free for God.

Last Saturday I announced that today we shall see what the Desert Fathers and St. Benedict taught about exaggerated self-love and self-will. I am sure that all of us have read and studied the sayings of some of the Desert Fathers, or read some of their lives.

I personally was struck by the manner in which the Desert Fathers condemned all manifestation of self-will. They say for instance: "Whoever prays sincerely, 'Thy will be done on earth as in heaven,' by no means may seek his own will, but should seek only the will of God."

Later Desert Fathers taught how necessary it is in every spiritual life, especially for a life as theirs, to combat seriously all capital vices, because they nourish self-will. As long as we are not free from our own vices, we are not masters of ourselves, nor are we free for God.

The Desert Fathers insisted on the necessity of having a Spiritual Father, doing nothing without his knowledge and permission.

Reading the lives and the sayings of the Desert Fathers, we get the following impressions:

1. that our own will is the greatest enemy to our spiritual progress and our sanctification;
2. that all we do when following our own will is suspect;
3. that we should always have the permission of our Spiritual Father for whatever we desire to do.

Rufinus, in his history of the monks, quotes the Great St. Anthony as saying: "Whoever desires to become perfect in a short time, by no means can be his own spiritual master, nor should he follow his own will, even if it seems to be the best thing to do." The reason is, says St. Anthony, that "following the teaching of our Divine Redeemer, in the first place, we should renounce ourselves and our will, imitating Our Lord who said: 'I did not come to do my own will, but rather the will of my Father, who sent me.'"

Let us now see, briefly, what St. Benedict said about our own will. In Chapter Four of the Holy Rule, St. Benedict, enumerating the tools of good works for a monk, says: "Renounce yourself in order to follow Christ; ...hate the urgings of self-will. Obey the orders of the Abbot unreservedly, even if his own conduct — which God forbid — be at odds with what he says. Remember the teachings of the Lord: 'Do what they say, not what they do' (Mt 23:3).... Do not love quarreling; shun arrogance."

St. Benedict in more than one place speaks about our will and teaches us that our will is our greatest enemy. "Truly, we are forbidden to do our own will," he says, and quoting the Holy Scripture he adds: "We are rightly taught not to do our own will since we dread what Scripture says: 'There are ways which men call right that in the end plunge into the depth of hell' (Prov 16:25)." [RB 7]

We shall come back to St. Benedict on another occasion and shall see that he established the monastic life for those who are willing to give up their own will and desire to live under holy obedience.

I hope [then to] finish our meditation upon the silence of our own will, for without that we are in opposition to the will of God and to holy obedience.

I repeat what was said already. Freedom and love are two great gifts we receive from God. They should help us to submit ourselves to God by personal decision, and conviction — of course with the help of God Himself — and to do the will of God out of deepest love for God and our neighbor.

Amen.

18

EXTERNAL SILENCE

Today we shall speak about external silence. We shall begin with the silence of the tongue, and continue with silencing all unnecessary and harmful noises.

As we should know, silence is not an end in itself, it is only a means to something better. No one is holy by the fact that he is not talking. Sometimes silence can become sinful and a privileged tool in the hands of the devil. Silence is sinful when it hurts the rights of others, when it lacks brotherly love, or when the devil asks us to hide something from our spiritual director or superior. Silence also becomes sinful if it is used for self-pity, bad thoughts, or rash judgments. If St. Benedict and all the Founders of Religious Orders or Congregations esteemed the value of silence, it is because they were convinced that the spirit of silence is a necessary and a most suitable means toward Christian perfection. Indeed, we cultivate silence to become more recollected and prayerful — to be both able to listen to the Holy Spirit and to converse with God.

For silence should never be void. It must be filled with prayer, with love, with God Himself. Through silence we should never become eccentric, but rather an image of God and His angels. Silence, of course, is also very useful for a perfect accomplishment of our work, study, and rest.

As far as we know, no religious had the presumption to introduce a perpetual silence or to forbid the use of the tongue always. It would not be pleasing to God, nor good for our human condition. We should respect God the Creator, and man, His creature. We should respect the gifts of God and the order established by God in His creatures. Saint Hildegard said: "It would be inhuman for men if they should always keep silence and never be allowed to speak."

In all religious families, psalms and other prayers have been recited publicly. All followed more or less the exhortation of St. Paul to the Colossians (3:16): "Sing gratefully to God from your hearts in psalms, hymns, and inspired songs." Also, in relation with their Superiors or with their Brothers, a moderate use of the tongue was always permitted to hermits, monks, and religious.

However, there has always been a limit in speaking or conversing with others. St. Benedict, in chapter six, quotes Psalm 38 (39) and the Book of Proverbs to convince his followers that they should be rather moderate in speaking, "Lest they should sin with their tongue." He says: "At times for the sake of silence we ought to refrain even from good words and much more from evil words, because in the multitude of words there shall not be want of sin." For this reason, St. Benedict says: "Let permission to speak be rarely given even to perfect disciples, even though their words be good and holy and conducive to edification, because the danger of sinning is always present (Prov 10:19); also, 'Death and life are in the power of the tongue' (Prov 18:21)."

St. James invites us to "be quick to hear," but "slow to speak." He continues: "If a man who does not control his tongue imagines that he is devout, he is self-deceived; his worship is pointless." (Jas 1:19-20, 26) St. James continues: "Always speak and act as men destined for judgment under the law of freedom. Merciless is the judgment on the man who has not shown mercy, but mercy triumphs over judgment." (2:12-13)

The law of freedom, just mentioned, is a law of love which man obeys freely and gladly, because to serve Christ means freedom. In the present situation of religious life in general, there are many practices of holy silence and many interpretations of its real value.

It seems that there is today a greater need for communication with others, a need of being together and enjoying each other. Also, we can see in some places, at least, a need for absolute withdrawal from human society. No doubt, in both tendencies there is something good. Indeed, we need communication with others, we need occasions to practice fraternal charity. In our life, such occasions are not lacking. Possibly, we do not always appreciate them rightly and, consequently, lose many merits before God and the occasion to be truly charitable.

If we withdraw in order to seek God and to come closer in union with Him — all is good. If we withdraw to seek ourselves, to seek our own interests and pleasures, if by withdrawing we close our heart to our Brothers, our attitude is at least suspect and possibly even sinful. Such an attitude could be harmful for the community as God's family, and for the individual religious by aggravating his psychological complexes. In all things there should be a healthy balance. There should be a time for everything as we read in the book of Ecclesiastes: "A time for giving birth; a time for dying; a time for planting and a time for uprooting what has been planted; ...a time for tears and a time for laughter; a time for mourning and a time for dancing; ...a time for keeping silent and a time for speaking." (Eccl 3:1-8)

In using occasions for speaking, let us be animated by both the spirit of discretion, so highly praised by St. Benedict, and by genuine Christian love. May the Holy Spirit teach us both — the love of silence and the love of our Brothers, especially when they are in need.

We should not only avoid idle talk [leading to] much laughter, as St. Benedict says, but we are also invited to avoid noisy behavior. Our Constitutions mention noisy manual work, disturbances during liturgical celebrations, and during the time of rest. Our Constitutions recommend silence in the church. We read in article 204: "Indiscreet turning of pages, coughing and impolite yawning should be avoided." [Reference is made here to what are now the former Constitutions, which were revised and rewritten in 1984.]

There are many ways of making noise. In my experience, I remember two of our Brothers who left the motor of the tractor running outside the door of the garage. Sometimes this kind of noise lasted for more than a half hour without reason. Others slam doors. Abbot [Paul] Delatte, in his commentary on St. Benedict's Rule[1] (p. 98), tells us that "a nun of the Visitation order asked St. Francis de Sales what she should do to reach perfection. The holy bishop, who doubtless knew whom he was addressing, replied: 'Sister, I think Our Lord wants you to close doors quietly.'"

Let us try to avoid all unnecessary noise, all impatient and distracting movements in whatever we do.

Next Saturday, once again, and possibly for the last time during these conferences, we shall speak about silence.

Msgr. Escriva de Balaguer says: "Silence is the door-keeper of the interior life." He adds: "After seeing how many people waste their lives (talking and talking), I can better appreciate how necessary and lovable silence is — and I can well understand, Lord, why you will make us account for every idle word."

Amen.

---

[1]   *The Rule of Saint Benedict*, The Archabbey Press, Latrobe, 1959.

19

SILENCE OF THE CAMALDOLESE

Today we shall speak briefly about our Camaldolese silence. Whoever approaches a hermitage of the Congregation of Montecorona is agreeably surprised by the spirit of silence and recollection which reigns there. Indeed, a Camaldolese hermitage is an oasis of peace and silence in the midst of a turbulent world.

St. Romuald (c. 950/2-1027), from his early years, searched for solitude and silence. His biographer, St. Peter Damian, wrote: "Whenever he was able to come upon a delightful place in the woods, his soul would at once be inflamed with a desire for a hermitage." Ever since, through all the centuries, and even down to the most recent foundations in the United States of America and Colombia, our hermitages have been situated on a hill surrounded by a dense forest. Far from the noise of towns and cities, far from highways and industrial centers, our hermitages have preserved the precious charism of St. Romuald — his love for solitude, silence, and austerity of life. We know well that solitude, silence, and fasting, in the mind of St. Romuald, were the means for something greater and more important: namely, a perfect love of God and neighbor, and that they led to a life of deep contemplative prayer. Means are not ends, but in our way of life they are necessary and powerful. A Camaldolese hermitage without the spirit or love for deep solitude and silence would be a contradiction indeed.

Bl. Paul Giustiniani (1476-1528), Reformer of the Camaldolese

Order and the Founder of our Congregation, wrote: "Silence is the principal adornment of solitude" [Constitutions of 1524]; "The silence of religious solitary life was not instituted to make us dumb animals, but to enable us to cease external conversation and to speak constantly to God in prayer or to speak usefully to ourselves in meditation. That is the meaning of religious silence: never to cease praying and meditating..."; also: "Silence is the condition of true solitude. Without silence there is no solitude" [autograph manuscripts]. [See *Alone with God*, by Dom Jean Leclercq, Chapter VI, where footnotes 9,10 & 12 are indicated. As there are several editions of the book now in print, the chapter reference applies to all editions, whereas page numbers all differ.]

Today, Camaldolese have no TV, no radio, no music, no secular newspapers; but we know from experience that our Camaldolese silence, being strict, is also wisely moderated. There are times when silence should not be dispensed, as for instance on Fridays, or during the two monastic Lents before Christmas and Easter. There are other occasions when silence may be dispensed and when the whole eremitical family comes together for a common meal or a walk. As a rule, our hermits should avoid all conversation with laymen, but they are permitted to converse among themselves as allowed by our Constitutions and customs. There is a great sobriety and a healthy balance in our Camaldolese way of life — alternating periods of silence and times of brotherly conversation. There is room for those who are called to absolute silence, in reclusion, but there is room for those who need more human contact with their brother hermits. It is obvious that relaxation of fervor will never be tolerated in our hermitages. But also, there is wise provision for interpersonal relationships and for Christian brotherly love.

Let us keep in mind what was said in our previous conferences about interior and exterior silence.

A hermit, who is able by God's grace to create in himself a good balance and bring to silence all voices and tendencies which are an obstacle to the action of the Holy Spirit in his soul, will have no great difficulties in becoming a man of silence and deep contemplative prayer. He also will be a man of radiant joy and great love. What is certain is this: having brought to silence all external and internal senses and all disorder coming from the intellectual faculties, a hermit will be free and willing to accept all the rigors of the solitary life and wholeheartedly embrace the monastic vows. He will remain faithful to his commitment to God and to the Church. Helped by the power of God, he will persevere to the end, animated by good zeal and great generosity. When the last hour arrives, joyfully awaited with deep peace of mind and heart, he will repeat with Simeon: "Lord, now let your servant go in peace, your word has been fulfilled." (Lk 2:25 ff)

Thank you for your attention and patience.

May Almighty God bless you, the Father, † the Son, and the Holy Spirit.

Amen.

20

CONCLUDING CONFERENCE

We take up silence again. It is our last conference on this subject. Much can still be said: for instance, how to keep our passions under control, and also our emotions and similar things. Today I would like to mention some practical points as a consequence and a conclusion to what has been said in previous conferences.

Silence is the result of a long ascetical program performed seriously and deliberately under the guidance of the Holy Spirit. Silence is not an instant product, something achieved quickly or without sacrifice. On the contrary, many sacrifices are necessary to bring to silence all the voices of our fallen nature, our personal vices, our likes and dislikes. Silence cannot be obtained without the spirit of mortification. Indeed, there is a great need for a mortified soul and a mortified body in order to follow the Crucified Christ.

If we have the tendency to dominate others, let us begin seriously to dominate first of all ourselves with our passions, our emotions, our weaknesses, our likes and dislikes. If we are anxious to see others more perfect than they are, let us begin with ourselves to become more perfect, more charitable, more Christ-like.

If we have the tendency to speak about poverty and the oppression of the poor, let us begin with ourselves to become more poor in spirit and in deeds. I have seen people who spoke highly about poverty and criticized others for not being poor enough, but who themselves were not always satisfied with things they were given! Very often they asked for exceptions and expressed special needs, which others did not have. They spoke about poverty, but wasted many things carelessly. For example, their bills for electricity often were the highest. This is not the poverty of Bethlehem.

Yes, love for the poor is a very good thing, but it does not dispense us from the obligation to become poor in spirit and in reality. We are called to follow the poor Christ in order to live according to the Beatitude: "Blessed are the poor in spirit, theirs is the kingdom of heaven." (Mt 5:3)

If we have the tendency to correct others, then let us reflect a while and ask ourselves: Do I not have the same vice or imperfection which I see in my brother? Then, inspired by the word of our Lord, let us correct ourselves. "Why do you observe the splinter in your brother's eye, and never notice the plank in your own? How dare you say to your brother: 'Let me take the splinter out of your eye,' when all the time there is a plank in your own?'" (Mt 7:3-4)

Some people feel inclined to convert the world, yet their own soul is not really converted, not living fully according to the law of Christ. "For what does it profit a man if he gain the whole world and suffer the loss of his own soul? Or what exchange shall a man give for his soul?" (Mt 16:26)

Let us also remember the words of St. Paul addressed to the Corinthians (13:1-3): "If I have the eloquence of men and of angels, but speak without love, I am simply a gong booming or a cymbal clashing. If I have the gift of prophecy, understanding all mysteries, and knowing everything, and if I have faith in all its fullness to move mountains, but am without love, then I am nothing at all."

Perfect silence in ourselves is the fruit of many sacrifices, of a long period of suffering, and of many tears and prayers.

Perfect silence is the sign of the final victory of Christ's power in our life. It is a great interior silence to which we are called — a silence filled with God.

The Holy Spirit is always busy in us, always helping us not to despair but to overcome all obstacles which impede the growth of Christ in our soul and in our life. Only Saints know what price must be paid, and of the many years, to reach the point of perfect silence in the soul.

Unfortunately, today the ascetical part of our spiritual life does not have many admirers, still less, followers. Many would like to reach the peak of perfection in a very short time, without any mortification or self-denial. To them it seems that love is all that is needed because it is the bond of perfection. What they say is correct but incomplete — they do not fully understand how many sacrifices are demanded by Christian love. We cannot really love God and our brothers if we do not die to ourselves. In order to love perfectly God and our neighbor, we must practically give up many things and accept making many sacrifices. Love asks for courageous and generous sacrifices! "Love must hurt us," said Mother Teresa of Calcutta.

St. Paul, in his First Letter to the Corinthians, does not hide that love is always patient and kind. As we know, both patience and kindness are the fruit of many sacrifices and self-denial. Love must also overcome jealousy and cannot be boastful or conceited. Love is never rude or selfish, is always ready to excuse, and to endure whatever comes. Whoever studies the meaning and qualities of love as presented in the Holy Scripture, must come to the conclusion that Christ must increase in me and I must decrease. We must die in order to live and to love perfectly. God has shown His infinite love for all through the Passion and death of Our Lord Jesus Christ on the Cross. Our love must be sealed by the cross. Love without sacrifices is not an authentic love.

"*Jesus autem tacebat*," "But Jesus was silent." (Mt 26:63) Jesus was arrested and brought before the Sanhedrin. There He was falsely accused. St. Matthew says: "The chief priests and the whole Sanhedrin were looking for evidence against Jesus, however false, on which they might pass the death sentence." How did Our Lord answer His accusers? St. Matthew tells us: "Jesus was silent."

May the silence of Jesus be our example and our inspiration. Let us follow the silent Master of whom Isaiah foretold (53:7): "Harshly dealt with, he bore it humbly, he never opened his mouth, like a lamb that is led to the slaughterhouse, never opening its mouth."

Accept and do what has been said in this and previous conferences. Even if we have human difficulties denying ourselves and dying to ourselves, it is what Christ asks us to do. Slowly but surely, with the help of God, we will overcome all difficulties, present and future, and will become perfectly free and happy.

May the Holy Spirit enlighten us and guide us. Let us not forget, however, that perfect love is the shortest way to real happiness.

Let us imitate Jesus and Mary, our models of silence.

Amen.

Biographical Note

These conferences were given at Holy Family Hermitage in 1986. The author died in 1996. They were edited by Holy Family Hermitage for publication in 2011, *cum permissu superiorum*.

Before becoming a Camaldolese, the author spent a quarter century as a missionary in Western Europe, far from his native land and acquainted with difficulties and dangers. The following episode was one of the more dramatic of those years.

In the early 1940's, he was serving as a hospital chaplain in France. It was the time of the turbulent German occupation and Gestapo terror.

One day, while on an upper floor of the hospital, he heard commotion below and looked down at the courtyard. It was filling up with storm troopers and Hitler youth. He rightly guessed that they had come to arrest everybody, and he also resolved not to surrender.

A soldier reached the upper-storey room, where the chaplain was, as the arrests were concluding. As he entered, he got a welcome he had not bargained for. The priest began to berate him, in perfect German, for his imperialism. "What? You speak German?" "Certainly, because when I was a boy, you occupiers made me go to a German school!" The dumbfounded soldier left the room without even attempting an arrest.

The chaplain again looked below and saw that the arrested were being loaded into vans, to be taken away to the death camps. He courageously rushed down and, as they were being driven off, gave them a blessing.

Years later, a woman who survived returned to thank him. "You'll never know how much that blessing meant to us!"

ERCAM EDITIONS
Holy Family Hermitage, Camaldolese Hermits of Montecorona

1. *Camaldolese Extraordinary:* The Life, Doctrine, and Rule of Blessed Paul Giustiniani, by Dom Jean Leclercq and Blessed Paul Giustiniani. Second edition, 2008, 460 pages. This fully indexed compendium includes Leclercq's *A Humanist Hermit* and *Alone with God*, Blessed Paul's *Rule* (abridged), and some shorter pieces.

2. *Camaldolese Spirituality:* Essential Sources, translation, notes, and introduction by Peter Damian Belisle. 2007, 267 pages. A unique resource comprising Saint Bruno Boniface's *Life of the Five Hermit Brothers*, Saint Peter Damian's *Life of Saint Romuald* and *Dominus Vobiscum*, and Blessed Rudolph's *Constitutions* and *Rule*.

3. *In Praise of Hiddenness:* The Spirituality of the Camaldolese Hermits of Montecorona, by a Camaldolese Hermit, edited by Father Louis-Albert Lassus, O.P. 2007, 108 pages. Spiritual conferences, plus a study of Saint Romuald, by an author who has spent more than thirty years in consecrated solitude.

4. *The Eremitic Life:* Encountering God in Silence and Solitude, by Father Cornelius Wencel, er. cam. 2007, 225 pages. A sketch of the hermit way of life for the general reader, by an accomplished Polish student of von Balthasar and contemporary theology.

5. *Alone with God:* First edition, 2008, 141 pages. Reprinted separately from *Camaldolese Extraordinary* by popular demand, this is the most famous work on the Camaldolese and the best introduction for the general reader.

For more information, visit www.Camaldolese.org

Printed in Great Britain
by Amazon.co.uk, Ltd.,
Marston Gate.